Praise

THE NE

T0012877

"Life is not the same after having children. It's delusional to pretend otherwise. But Mike Birbiglia and J. Hope Stein have not only survived, they're making their most hilarious and truthful art yet. This book might save your best friend's life."

—Lin-Manuel Miranda, Pulitzer
Prize–winning writer of *Hamilton*

"Mike Birbiglia and Jen Stein are the best collaborators since Emily Dickinson teamed up with her long-winded comedian friend. I'm joking because I cannot express how much this book affected me and how many times it made me cry."

—John Mulaney, comedian

"Mike Birbiglia and J. Hope Stein have written the seminal parenting tome—side-splittingly funny from the first word to the last delicious bite. It's a page-turner, wise and wise-assed, the comic hit of the year. Whether you've been a parent or ever had one: you'll love this knockout!"

—Mary Karr, author of
The Liars' Club, Cherry, and *Lit*

"The genius of this book is that Mike Birbiglia and J. Hope Stein have invented a totally new form. He tells incredibly funny stories. She gives a gorgeous, epic view of the same events, in poetry (she's a published poet who's been in *The New Yorker*). It's about what they went through together, not wanting to have kids, and then having kids, through these two very different lenses. Their diabolical writing trick: sometimes she delivers the laughs and he delivers the feelings."

—Ira Glass, host of Public Radio's
This American Life

"If *The New One* on Broadway is a raucous, tumbling tour through the many roomed house that is Mike and Jen's journey into parenthood, then this book is a long, cozy weekend inside the home. Mike makes you coffee and settles in to tell his story at a wonderfully readable pace, bringing detail and nuance impossible to contain in the stage show. Jen's poetry is the big stunner, an outrageous treasure casually presented, emeralds strewn amongst crumbs across the kitchen table, a string of pearls hanging on a doorknob."

—Jacqueline Novak, author of
How to Weep in Public

"Comedian, actor, director, and producer Mike Birbiglia explores his mixed feelings about becoming a parent. His confessional and observational prose passages are interspersed with lyrical interludes written by his wife, poet J. Hope Stein...A lighthearted and uncomfortable portrait of fatherhood."

—*Publishers Weekly*

"Sex, sympathy weight, and Birbiglia's sleep disorder are all fair game in this hilariously, sometimes shockingly, and always refreshingly honest look at having a kid and becoming new one's self."
—*Booklist*

"Seasoned and rookie dads alike will appreciate Birbiglia's comic riffs on family life. His memoir is a can't-miss gift that's sure to make 'em laugh."
—*Bookpage*

"Reading this raw and vulnerable book was almost like opening a page into Mike Birbiglia's diary; his emotion is truly refreshing. He is a wonderful comedian who will have you laughing and crying and thinking, all in the span of a single chapter."
—*Bookreporter*

The
NEW
ONE

PAINFULLY TRUE STORIES
from A RELUCTANT DAD

MIKE BIRBIGLIA
with POEMS by J. HOPE STEIN

GCP

GRAND CENTRAL
PUBLISHING

NEW YORK BOSTON

Copyright © 2020 by Mike Birbiglia
All poems © 2020 by J. Hope Stein

Cover art and design by Wendy MacNaughton and Crystal English Sacca
Cover copyright © 2021 by Hachette Book Group, Inc.

Hachette Book Group supports the right to free expression and the value of copyright. The purpose of copyright is to encourage writers and artists to produce the creative works that enrich our culture.

The scanning, uploading, and distribution of this book without permission is a theft of the author's intellectual property. If you would like permission to use material from the book (other than for review purposes), please contact permissions@hbgusa.com. Thank you for your support of the author's rights.

Grand Central Publishing
Hachette Book Group
1290 Avenue of the Americas, New York, NY 10104
grandcentralpublishing.com
twitter.com/grandcentralpub

Originally published in hardcover in May 2020 by Hachette Book Group.
First trade paperback edition: May 2021

Grand Central Publishing is a division of Hachette Book Group, Inc. The Grand Central Publishing name and logo is a trademark of Hachette Book Group, Inc.

The publisher is not responsible for websites (or their content) that are not owned by the publisher.

The Hachette Speakers Bureau provides a wide range of authors for speaking events. To find out more, go to www.hachettespeakersbureau.com or call (866) 376-6591.

Library of Congress Cataloging-in-Publication Data

Names: Birbiglia, Mike, author. | Stein, J. Hope (Jen Hope), author.
Title: The new one : painfully true stories from a reluctant dad / Mike Birbiglia ; with poems by J. Hope Stein.
Description: First edition. | New York : Grand Central Publishing, 2020. |
Identifiers: LCCN 2019049244 | ISBN 9781538701515 (hardcover) |
   ISBN 9781538701539 (ebook)
Subjects: LCSH: Birbiglia, Mike. | Birbiglia, Mike—Family. | Humorists, American—Biography. | Fatherhood—Humor. | Parent and child—Humor. | Parenting—Humor. | Parent and child—Poetry. | Parenting—Poetry.
Classification: LCC PN2287.B45463 A3 2020 | DDC 792.7/6028092 [B]—dc23
LC record available at https://lccn.loc.gov/2019049244

ISBNs: 978-1-5387-0151-5 (hardcover); 978-1-5387-0152-2 (trade paperback); 978-1-5387-0153-9 (ebook)

Printed in the United States of America

LSC-C

Printing 1, 2021

CONTENTS

The NEW ONE

THE BOOK STARTS HERE

In June of 2016 my wife, Jen, and I took our fourteen-month-old daughter, Oona, to the Nantucket Film Festival. When the festival director picked us up at the Nantucket airport (which was basically someone's backyard with planes in it), she asked if I would tell a story at the festival's storytelling night.

She said, "The theme is jealousy."

I said, "I don't think I want to tell a story."

Jen said, "You're jealous of Oona. You should talk about that."

There was a playfulness with which Jen was needling me, but also...she was right. The theme of the night could have been any number of things: "fear," "change," "fear of change," "loneliness." But the theme was jealousy. So that's where I began.

That afternoon I started opening up my journals and sharing with Jen some of my deepest, darkest, and funniest thoughts about our decision to have a child. Writing is always a process of trial and error, but this was writing about my own errors, so the errors felt compounded, like I was re-living my own mistakes and failing at that too. Jen and I shared with each other our sides of what had gone down during the pregnancy and in that first year with our daughter.

I told a story that week. It went pretty well. And so it began.

Over the next two years, Jen and I continued to write about this subject.

Our work evolved into an entire show called *The New One*, which ended up on Broadway.

The more I performed the show, the more people told me that

the stories gave them a sense of catharsis—not just parents but also people who resist all kinds of change. So I pored over my journals, dug deeper, found a lot more stories, and created this book: *The New One: Painfully True Stories from a Reluctant Dad.* The book became something I had never expected to write. I confessed things to the page that I was previously uncomfortable confessing to myself. As I worked on the book, Jen showed me some poetry she was writing about the same themes. That poetry is sprinkled through these pages (those are my favorite parts).

So here it is. We hope you enjoy it. This book is an experiment. We figured it out as we went along.

Sort of like a family.

little astronaut

a newborn rests her head on the earth of mother.
everything else is outer space.

—J. Hope Stein

ZOMBIE KID-POCALYPSE

My brother, Joe, used to be so cool, then he had two kids and now he's a loser.

Well, he's not a loser, but I will say his house is a lot less fun. Not that my life is that much more *fun*. It's just that I'm comfortable. I live in Brooklyn with my wife, Jen, and our cat, Mazzy, and we have long decided that we are not going to have kids. It's one of the things Jen and I have always had in common. Sometimes we drive away from visiting our friends who have kids and confide in each other, "Fuck that," from the privacy of our crumb-free sedan.

It's fall of 2012 when I wake up on Joe's couch. I'm trudging through his living room, tripping over stuffed pigs and Pack 'n Plays, and I join Joe's family in the kitchen.

I open the fridge and grab a jar of peanut butter, and there is peanut butter on the outside of the jar. So I'm holding a jar of peanut butter covered in peanut butter. And I think, *How the hell did this happen? Did someone grab a handful of peanut butter out of the jar with their hand and then rub it on toast? And where might that person with that lack of judgment also put that same hand?* I toss the peanut butter back in the fridge and sit at the table with Joe and the kids. Joe's older son, Henry, is five. His younger son is two. The two-year-old is named Merritt, which was a name awarded to him at birth after he had achieved no accomplishments whatsoever.

I plop down at the table across from Joe and his meritless children. The moment my butt strikes the chair, I realize that I'm resting on a sticky yogurt pouch. I look around for a napkin but the table is covered in wet Cheerios and Aquaphor, which are, I believe, the opposite of napkins. I look to my left, where Joe is queuing up a video on his phone of his son Henry. I find this infuriating. I think, *I have Henry live. I don't need Henry on tape.*

The video itself: underwhelming. Joe says, "This is a video of Henry picking apples. Make sure you watch until the end!"

I say, "When does it end?"

He says, "It's about twelve minutes long."

I think, *Nobody wants to watch that. There's so much great content out there. I was on YouTube and I saw a ninety-second video of a cat giving another cat a massage. Don't waste my time with "Henry picking apples."*

Joe elaborates on their apple-picking trip. Something about stopping for ice cream on the way home. He fishes around in his phone for photo documentation, which I had not requested.

Joe says, "This is the best photo. It's Henry eating ice cream!"

I think, *This is a terrible photograph. The lighting is garish. The framing is so tight that I can't even tell he's eating ice cream.*

I sit at the breakfast table doing my best to facially express supportive disinterest, and Joe presses on like an air traffic controller on his first day of work.

He says, "Henry ate ice cream even though he hates cold things!"

I think, *People with children don't know how to tell stories. That's not a story. That's a "detail" in a story. Stories have a beginning, middle, and end. What you said is a boring, boring, and a boring, basted in boring sauce and baked at 200 degrees for ninety seconds. At best, it's a middle. It's a middle where you're thinking, "Get to the end!" But there is no end. Or beginning. It's just this constant flow of "middle."*

Joe hops up to grab orange juice from the fridge. He's barely recognizable. This person was never supposed to become a dad. He was too cool to be a dad. He had introduced me to Public Enemy and Nirvana. He taught me how to dance alone in my room to Talking Heads and write jokes and ski off cliffs and smoke pot. Everything I knew about cool through age twenty was mainlined through Joe. Even when our sisters went off to college we continued to share a bedroom and a boom box and a dream, and his having children felt like a betrayal—like he had forgotten about all the rad stuff we had done together and caved to this mediocre grown-up existence. He was like a marathon runner who, at mile nineteen, is handed a backpack full of boulders. I don't mean to equate children with boulders, but I couldn't come up with a heavy, useless item that also plays video games and eats candy.

To be fair: Maybe I have a low tolerance for children because I've lost a lot of great friends to kids. Because parenting really *is* like a disease. But it's worse than a disease because they want you to have it too. They say things like, "You should have kids too!" And I think, *I'm watching you do it and I'm thinking I'm gonna not do it.*

They're like zombies, hissing, "Youuuuu should eeeaaaat brains!!!"

I'm watching you eat brains and it seems like it ruined your life.

The way you kill zombies (you probably know this from the movies) is you shoot 'em in the head with a shotgun or chop off their heads with a machete or a samurai sword, which is also the way you kill anyone.

I'm sitting with my zombie brother and his family eating peanut butter Puffins when Henry starts whacking me in the head with a foam bat.

I say, "What *game* is this?!" and I look over to Joe for assistance.

Joe does nothing. He's like a World Wrestling referee. He says, "He's not supposed to do that."

I hobble away from the table and duck inside the bathroom. I try to pee, but the toilet has that childproof circle-inside-the-circle-inside-the-circle. Like a carnival peeing game that I'm losing badly. Henry kicks in the door and now I'm peeing into the wall, which has pee on it already.

I lock the door.

I stand there for fifteen minutes doing nothing other than avoiding Joe's family. I pull out my phone and search for local activities. I exit the bathroom and say, "Joe, we should see this band at the Paradise."

Joe says, "I can't go to a concert, Mike. I have kids!"

I say, "Sorry."

Joe says, "Don't apologize. It's the most joy I've ever experienced."

I say, "Congratulations on your ambiguous tone!"

We don't go out. We stay home and watch these Baby Einstein videos, which have yielded no geniuses, to my knowledge. There's nothing about the theory of relativity in the one I saw. It was just a pig playing a xylophone and then a dog barks and a lady says, "Pillow!" and then my nephew spits yogurt on his shirt.

That's when Joe confides in me: "He's a genius."

I think, *I'm not seeing it, man, but sure, maybe he's a genius.*

I fall asleep that night at 7:30 p.m. because being around children makes me want to be unconscious at all times. I wake up at 4:30 a.m. with a fierce cold from sleeping in this petri dish house and a ringing foam bat headache. I stumble into a cab and hobble onto my flight and all I can think is *I just want to be home with my wife and my cat and my couch.*

To be clear: I love my wife and my cat, but I also love my couch.

It's the first thing I ever dropped money on in my life. In your twenties you just *get* a couch on the street—which is a great price. It's literally garbage, this mysterious lump of wood and fabric, and you bring it home to your six roommates and they're like, "Nice."

But then I reached an age—I was twenty-five years old and living in Astoria, Queens—and I thought, *I'm a goddamned man. I'm gonna buy a goddamned couch.* And I went to a department store and sat on what I believed to be the least expensive couch and then gasped when I looked at the price tag. I said to the clerk, "Wait, this one's a thousand dollars?"

"Yes, it is," he said.

"Is there gonna be a sale?"

"This is the sale."

"Do you think you might go out of business?"

"We are going out of business."

I think the reason a couch is so expensive is that it's a deceptively sophisticated piece of technology. It's a bed that hugs you.

A couch is accommodating: *You wanna watch TV? You wanna eat pizza? You sure do like eating. But I like that about you!*

Meanwhile, beds are comfy but they know it: *I'd like to be called a king. I'm gonna need a box spring. I don't touch the floor. Get your hands off that tag! I'd like this room named after me.*

Couches are humble: *This is about you. You wanna take a nap? Be my guest. You wanna have sex with my arm? I'll think about it.*

In 2008, Jen and I got married at city hall in New York City, which is a great place to get married if you have the chance. Very convenient. We took the subway home. We took selfies on the subway. We ate pizza and hamburgers at this place in our neighborhood called Big Nick's. And then we took a nap—on the couch.

And since then we've spent thousands of hours together on this couch. We've watched classic films on the couch. We've eaten twenty birthday cakes on the couch. We've laughed hysterically on the couch. We've cried on the couch in each other's arms when we found out we had to put our cat Ivan to sleep. It's soft, yet firm. Filthy, yet spotless. Colorful, yet no one can agree on what color it is. I think it's green. Jen thinks it's gray. I looked it up—chocolate. Which isn't a color but feels fitting because there's chocolate *in it.*

I love being home on my couch, but I travel for my job. I perform comedy in sometimes a hundred cities in a year—which is more cities than there are.

Some of them are just an Applebee's with a dream.

I love performing, but the travel can be rigorous. And often when I return home I feel entirely empty—just bones and garbage and Diet Coke held together by those plastic ringlets that bind sodas and strangle ducks. I smell like a rental car filled with Pop-chip farts, Cinnabon wrappers, and Febreze. My breath smells like fast-food barbecue sauce. I use the last drop of caffeine in my veins to push my body across the finish line that is my doorstep, and I collapse on our beloved couch...

And it hugs me.

I say to my wife, "Clo..." (Her name is Jen.) "Leave me by the side of the road."

But she doesn't.

She revives me.

Jen has a soft, sweet voice. It has a thread count of six hundred. It's a voice that always seems like it's telling you a secret or saying, "I'm gonna make tea."

Jen and I lie on the couch and she orders me a chicken kebab platter and scratches my back, and we snuggle with our cat, Mazzy, and watch a documentary about murder.

And that's what love is.

And it all takes place...

On the couch.

I meditate on this couch/cat fantasy as I squeeze into my Jet-Blue seat. I notice a baby across the aisle screaming at the top of his lungs. And in that moment, and I can't defend this, but I think, *That baby doesn't need to be anywhere. I'm wearing noise-canceling headphones. Which apparently aren't enough. You need baby...canceling...headphones, which are...condoms...I guess. We gotta get babies off planes. We got rid of smoking in the eighties, we could get rid of babies now. Or bring back smoking and get these babies some cigarettes because they're so stressed out.*

After an hour that feels like ten, I land in New York and take a cab to our apartment. I melt into our beloved couch and it hugs me.

I say, "Clo [her name is Jen]—people with kids are miserable."

Jen laughs.

And I laugh.

We laugh as one.

Then she says: "But if we had a baby, I think it would be different."

I inch away from the couch, spooked as though I had seen something supernatural but knowing that what I'm seeing is perhaps the most natural life progression of all.

I whisper to myself, "She got bit."

I return to the couch and speak with the professional calm of an FBI agent during a hostage crisis. This is my Waco. I say, "Clo—I was *very clear* when we got married that I never wanted to have a kid."

Which, by the way, gets you nothing. Being *very clear* is apparently useless.

She says, "I was very clear that I didn't want to have a baby at the time but that I might change."

I say, "I was clear that I would never change."

She says, "If you don't want to have a baby, maybe I'll have one on my own and we can stay married."

I say, "That'll be a good look. Just you and me and this kid that's a cross between you and some grad student jacking his way through SUNY Purchase. You can't just have a kid on the side. You can't tell the neighbors, 'It's fine! We keep him in the shed!' People do it, I've seen the documentaries, but those aren't my role models."

Jen says, "A baby wouldn't have to change the way we live our lives."

I say, "Did you get less smart? You used to be so smart. You're a poet. You're a deep thinker, and what you're saying right now is factually incorrect. It wouldn't change the way we live our lives except for the part of my life where I fundamentally don't want to have a child, which is all of it. Do you really want another me? Just this miniature fidgety, loudmouthed, attention-starved sleepwalker?"

Jen says, "The baby won't be like you. The baby will be like me. Quiet and shy. Like a cat who reads books."

I say, "Clo, first of all, cats can't read."

Jen says, "No one knows for sure."

There's a long pause.

Too long.

A unique detail about being married to a poet is that often she'll say one line, and then there's a lot of space.

I've never wanted to have a kid for seven specific reasons.

I.

SEVEN REASONS

1

I LOVE MY MARRIAGE

I feel lucky to have found my wife.

I never thought I'd meet anyone who'd put up with me. I thought I'd find someone who would pretend to be okay with me and then try to change me, fail, and then divorce me. But that didn't happen. Jen *loves me back*. One time Jen was rubbing my neck and I said, "Do I feel more tense than usual?" and Jen said, "You've been 80 to 100 percent tense since the day we met." And I thought, *She really gets me.*

When Jen and I first met, our work schedules didn't match. Jen worked nine to six in an office building overlooking the Hudson. I was on the road about 70 percent of the time doing shows. To make matters worse, when I was in New York City, I was performing at night. So I...stay with me...showed up at her job every day without an invitation—for two and a half weeks.

In current times this would be called "stalking." At the time it was called "stalking." I wouldn't recommend this tactic unless you are completely willing to go to jail and/or get married.

So I would show up at Jen's work every day with flowers and I'd pop into the conference room or her office.

Jen would be mortified. She'd whisk me outside to Pier 60 and we would make out on the promenade. The first time this happened, Jen's phone dropped out of her pocket mid-kiss.

*

Prank Calls from Fish

The first time my husband kissed me my cellphone fell
out of my pocket into the Hudson River and to this day
I still receive prank calls from fish.

*

Jen is a poet. She's always published under a pseudonym. It's
"Allen Ginsberg."

Actually, it's "J. Hope Stein," but I've coaxed Jen into revealing
her pseudonym for this book, which means she plans to switch
to a new, even more secret-y pseudonym upon its publication. So
good luck tracking that down. Jen is very private. Until now she
has never shared her pseudonym with family or friends, which I
find maddening, so I created a pseudonym of my own who is an
online superfan of her pseudonym and writes love letters to her
pseudonym.

His name is Embir Bones. I've created a Gmail address for
Embir Bones, and I write J. Hope Stein emails from that account.
At one point I sent flowers from Embir Bones to J. Hope Stein
and my follow-up email read:

Did u get the flowers? Was that ok w ur husband? I googled
him. He's a comedian. I've never heard of him. You need to
lose that zero and get down with Embir.

Jen replied:

Mr. Bones,

Yes, I did get your flowers—beautiful! My cat Mazzy especially
loves them since they remind her of when she was a street cat.

My husband is very secure in our relationship.

Sincerely,

J. Hope Stein

I don't mean to belabor this point, but a pseudonym has always seemed absurd to me. If I wrote poems as beautifully as she does, I would buy a billboard in Times Square that said CHECK OUT THESE FUCKING POEMS.

But she doesn't.

Jen's publishing philosophy:

*

you can publish when you're dead,
                                    says the tree.

*

One night Jen came home from a poetry reading. I asked her how it went and she said, "There was no microphone and because my voice is so quiet, no one could hear me."

So for our first anniversary, I bought her a microphone and portable amplifier to bring to her readings. On the box I placed a card that read "Dear Clo, Your voice needs to be heard."

I am obsessed with Jen's voice, and I'm one of the few people who gets to hear it.

Jen is an introvert.

I am an extrovert.

An extrovert is someone who gets energy from being around other people, and an introvert doesn't like you.

Well, she might like you, but her husband will have to explain why we're leaving the party. That's my role in our marriage. I'm Jen's social bodyguard. When Jen is socially past her point, I need to come up with an immediate excuse for us to leave, and often the excuses are less than convincing. For example, I blurt, "WE HAVE A CAT!" and then we exit.

I didn't enter the marriage as an extrovert. I was an introvert who, when married to an even deeper introvert, was forced to find my inner extrovert. Someone had to. Otherwise how would we leave the party?

Whenever I make these excuses to leave social events, I can see a certain look on the listener's face. I'm not fluent in face, but it's something like, *This guy is an asshole.*

And that may be, but it doesn't take away from the fact that I am an excellent social bodyguard for my wife, who is a quiet and shy cat who reads books.

Jen is truly one of a kind. Nearly every aspect of Jen is anomalous. I travel for my job and *she likes it when I'm away.* I get tickets to cool events, she *likes to stay home.* She *likes salad.* She's not eating it as a punishment for eating pizza. She *enjoys lettuce as food.* Solitude is her oxygen and salad is her sunlight.

Which is all to say—*I love my marriage.*

And I'm not saying it's perfect. I think all marriages have an undercurrent of tension at all times because you have two people experiencing many of the same events at the same time, and then you have *two completely different memories of the same event.*

A few years ago we were in a hotel elevator in Chicago, and I remembered that on the lobby level there was a café that Jen had loved a few years before.

I said, "I just remembered you loved the café at this hotel!"
Jen said, "Who did?"
And I thought, *Oh no.*
Because the subtext of "Who did?" was:

A. That wasn't me.
B. That was another woman you were dating.
C. I'm not happy about this.

We got to the lobby, and the elevator doors opened and Jen said, "Oh, yeah. I love this café!"

And I thought, *I nearly died in the elevator. I almost had a heart attack two minutes ago and you just casually remembered that I was right.*

So now—whenever we have a shared memory that isn't exactly the same—one of us says the phrase "Who did?" which is our way of saying, "We're both probably wrong."

I love my marriage.

And I don't fall for those wedding clichés where people say, "Two become one." But I do feel like, if you're lucky in a relationship, there are *moments*...and I mean...*moments.*

Like, *this* is a moment...

That was a moment.

There are *moments* where you feel as if your souls are colliding in a way that no two souls have collided in the history of humankind. And you think, *How did I get this lucky?*

Jen and I hate going to parties, but we love *driving away from parties*. A few years ago we went to our friend Katie's birthday and this lady got up and gave a speech, which isn't a thing. That's why I remember it so well. She said, "Last year Katie and I went scuba diving and her oxygen tank got stuck on the rocks and I wriggled it free and I may have saved her life. I saved your best friend's life." Jen and I locked eyes from across the room and telepathically projected the sentence:

We're gonna talk about this for years.

And we have.

Here's how it comes up. Whenever Jen and I do something sweet for each other. Like, for example, I have a serious sleepwalking disorder that requires me to sleep in a sleeping bag (more on that later). Anyway, sometimes she'll zip me up in the sleeping bag and she'll say, "It's time to put you in your pod."

I'll say, "Thanks."

And she'll say, "I saved your best friend's life."

It's never not funny. It has literally never not been funny. I don't want to give that up. I don't want that to change. I don't want a third person showing up and saying, "What about me?!"

I'd say, "We don't even know you!"

Which is all to say I'm married to someone who gets prank calls from fish and has visited a special little café in Chicago *twice* whether she remembers it or not. I'm married to the Clark Kent of poetry who has saved my best friend's life and for many years shared with me the solidarity that we would never have children. I didn't want to lose that. I didn't want that to change.

2

MY BODY IS A LEMON

I've never felt that there should be more of me in the world. Don't get me wrong, I think one of me is funny. But I believe in survival of the fittest, and I am not the fittest. I have the body of someone who's just about to embark on a robust exercise regimen and then doesn't.

And I also have a long medical history. I had a malignant tumor in my bladder when I was nineteen. I was lucky. The doctors caught the tumor early, took it out, and it hasn't come back, but every year I'm reminded of it because I go for what's called a cystoscopy, where a doctor takes a rod that's about as long as a tennis racket and as thick as a Twizzler with a camera on the end, and he sticks it through your urethra to look into your bladder... *while you're awake.*

Or I should say, "While *other people* are awake." I get knocked out for it.

But I didn't that first time. When I was twenty, my urologist, Dr. Kaplan, put me in a chair with those leg stirrups and he applied a local anesthetic and some jelly that was quite cold. The moment the scope made contact with my body, I shouted. Dr. Kaplan seemed shocked. Not concerned but shocked. And all I could think was, *You stuck a meat thermometer into my penis and you didn't think I was gonna shout? Who is your clientele?*

But Dr. Kaplan was unfazed. He said, "Relax ya butt!"

And I said, "*You* relax *your* butt!"

By the way, if you ever find yourself in a situation where you need to convince someone to relax their butt, one thing I'd suggest *not* saying is "relax your butt." I think it has almost a reversing quality. If butt relaxation is your endgame, maybe throw a curveball like "relax your ears!" The person might get distracted and think, *Hey, my butt feels pretty loose!* and then whatever you're trying to get into that person's butt will just slide right in there.

Which is all to say: I get knocked out for this annual procedure.

Last year was particularly eventful because I had gone for my physical and, since I was nearing forty, they suggested a prostate exam, which, you probably know, is a finger in the butt and one in your mouth if you're close with the physician. (That's what I was told.)

But I couldn't handle it. My doctor went for it and I politely dodged his finger and said, "Oh, no thank you!"

So, before I went for my annual cystoscopy, I said to Dr. Kaplan, "Hey, while I'm under, would you mind *also* sticking your finger in my butt?"

Dr. Kaplan replied, as though I had asked him to pass the salt, "Yeah, I can do that."

I thought, *I might be a medical genius. I never went to school for this, I barely finished* Our Bodies, Ourselves, *and I just invented the urology twofer. Which, if it catches on, should be renamed "the Birbiglia Bonus."*

So I had cancer. I have a life-threatening sleepwalking disorder. I wrote a book about it called *Sleepwalk with Me*. I even made a movie out of that, but just because you make a movie about something doesn't mean it's cured. If you haven't read or seen *Sleepwalk with Me*, it's based on a true-life incident thirteen years ago where I sleepwalked through a second-story window at a La Quinta Inn in Walla Walla, Washington. When I say "through" I mean *through the glass*. I dreamed I was on a ship and there was a guided missile that was targeting me. In order to save all the people in the boat, I sprinted towards the window (in my dream and, as it turns out, in real life) and smashed *through the glass.* I landed on the front lawn, took a fall, got up, and kept running! And I lived—which is why it is humorous now.

I actually drove myself to a hospital in Walla Walla and got thirty-three stitches in my leg. A shard of glass was a centimeter from my femoral artery and, had it struck the artery, I could have bled out on the front lawn of the motel and died. I was diagnosed with a rare condition called REM sleep behavior disorder, so now, every night when I go to bed, I take a very strong narcotic and then slide myself into a sleeping bag and wear mittens so I can't open the sleeping bag.

And that's my life!

There are details in my life that are both setups and punch lines. My sleep physician recently explained to me that, had I been killed in the incident in Walla Walla, the police would have classified the death as a "pseudo-suicide." It's a deeply terrifying feeling when your subconscious and conscious mind have diametrically opposed goals.

I make a lot of jokes about my sleepwalking, but it's a very serious condition. There are people with this disorder who have, in rare instances, been known to kill the person they're in bed with while remaining asleep.

I don't think *that's* a great quality in a dad.

So I had cancer. I act out my dreams. My health isn't trending upward. Last year when I went for my physical my doctor took blood and he called me with the results and said, "You're prediabetic, you have high cholesterol, *and* you have Lyme disease."

I thought, *One at a time! Everybody's gonna get a chance!*

My doctor put me on antibiotics for the Lyme disease. Then, regarding the diabetes, he said, "Is there anything in your diet that might be spiking your blood sugar?"

I said, "Sometimes I eat pizza until I'm unconscious."

He said, "I think that might be it."

So I had Lyme disease, I'm prediabetic, I'm generally devoid of joy.

I really am.

Sometimes I'll watch these action movies, but I don't relate to the hero, which I think is sort of the idea. I relate to that other guy. The buddy. The guy who gets shot and then the hero says, "Stay awake, bro!" But I don't want to stay awake.

I make a lot of jokes about sleepwalking, but it really is a battle for me to get out of bed in the morning because I take Klonopin, which knocks you the hell out. It can cause "paranoid or suicidal ideation and impair memory, judgment, and coordination. Combining with other substances, particularly alcohol, can slow breathing and possibly lead to death." Other than that, it's great.

I once asked my doctor if I could stop taking the Klonopin because of the dangerous side effects and daily hangover, and he said, "Look, Mike, you jumped through a window in your sleep. You've made your sleeping bag."

Point taken, nerd.

But I hate these meds because the hangover is fierce. When I saw the film *Memento*, in which handsome Guy Pearce wakes up every morning with no memory of his own life and follows a series of prompts he's written for himself on Post-it notes, it felt like my own documentary. Except instead of handsome Guy Pearce it's drowsy and pudgy Mike Birbiglia tripping over everything in his path. The first forty-five minutes of my day are like an electronic doll down to its final 3 percent of battery life. My words are slurred, my body is in slow motion, a single sock hangs off my foot. The rest of my day is spent thinking about where I've gone wrong.

Half of the time I feel empty. A quarter of the time I feel… okay. I never feel full. I don't have enough gas in the tank for *passengers*. I'm constantly refilling with coffee, the liquid false promise that joy is on the way.

I try to experience joy. I listened to this TED Talk about how to find joy and the speaker, Ingrid Fetell Lee, said that one thing everyone enjoys is confetti.

And I thought, *I hate confetti.* To me confetti is just garbage you throw into the air. That doesn't seem positive.

So I sleepwalk.

I had cancer.

Lyme disease.
I'm prediabetic.
I have high cholesterol.
I dislike joy.
I'm not exactly handing off A-plus genes here.

3

I DON'T KNOW ANYTHING

I'm not ready to "teach the children."

I've read hundreds of books; I've retained very little. In third grade they taught us photosynthesis and I thought, *This is not gonna stick.*

It hasn't.

I'm not 100 percent sure why it rains.

My brain is like a Snapple cap. It can hold one piece of information at a time.

I can't even snap my fingers.

I don't know anything for certain. I think it's entirely possible that consciousness is a hallucination. How do I explain that to a kid?

"Hey, kid, see that juice box? Don't be so sure."

I can't explain existence. I was raised Catholic, but I didn't really believe in God. I believed in my mom, and my mom believed in God. It was like I was in this weird three-way with God where I thought, *It's okay if he's here while you're here, but I'm not gonna do anything with just me and him.* To be clear, I've never had sex with my mom. Or God. Or had a three-way. So it's a true metaphor.

I had so many questions in Catholic school, but that only made it worse. In sixth grade I asked Sister Kathy, "What happens in heaven?"

She said, "Heaven is whatever you want it to be."

I thought, *That's just me masturbating all the time.*

She also pointed out that "God is always watching us," and I thought, *He must be watching me do that too.*

So I would try to cheat to the camera. I wanted to give God a good angle. I always thought if he happened to glance at the monitor at that moment, I would want him to think, *I've seen a lot of twelve-year-olds masturbate, but this kid is good.* I had so many questions as a kid and what I probably needed was therapy, but Catholics don't believe in therapy. They believe in confession, which is a cross between therapy and a glory hole.

I don't go to church anymore, but every once in a while I'll pray. Mostly when I'm in a jam. I never pray when things are going well. When things are going my way, I think, *I am God!* To be clear, I don't assume the prayers will work. I think of prayers like tech support. Unless I get a person live on the phone, I'm not sure it's getting to anyone. And if you do get someone live to answer your prayers, that's when you know you're dreaming, or dead.

And maybe what they taught me in Catholic school was true. But ultimately anyone exercising faith in any religion is just *guessing*, and you have to assume that some people are *guessing wrong*. I think God might exist, but I'm pretty sure he's not a white dude with a beard. If God is white, how do you explain Asia? Or Africa? I don't remember the passage in the Bible where God said, "I shall make you in my image and likeness, except you four billion." If God is white he has an Asian fetish.

I don't go to church, but I regularly attend the Museum of Natural History. I know that's not considered a holy place, but at least they have fossils. If church had fossils of Peter, Paul and Mary (the folk trio or the saints), I would think, *This story checks out.* But the Museum of Natural History displays these massive fossils held together by some kind of dinosaur crazy glue. And even with fossils on display they don't claim to know the absolute truth.

One time Jen and I were at the Museum of Natural History staring at this dinosaur skull that was the size of a small motorcycle and we noticed this sign underneath that said "These are all intriguing hypotheses, but the fossils do not give us enough evidence to test whether any of them are correct. The mystery remains unresolved." And I thought, *Come on, guys, give yourselves a little credit here! You found the giant dino skull and the giant dino leg bones and the dino arms, all in the dino shape in the side of some mountain in Montana. You've shown your work!* We need that "mystery remains unresolved" placard over there on the Bible, and the Koran, and the Book of Mormon.

Can't we agree that all religions are just hunches? We should rename religions "hunches." As in: "Which hunch do you belong to?" "I'm of the Catholic hunch. We have this hunch that the son of God came to earth and died for our sins so that he could open the gates of heaven."

Which is part of why I never wanted to have a kid. I don't think my hunch is better than yours.

*

littlefishnobody

for a third grade science project
i monitored the movements of fish
as i played for them several genres of music
and observed: there is a swish

in the hips of woman and man
that moves back and forth and back and forth
and back—all the way back
to our ancestors the fish.

but i am nothing as useful as a lover
or scientist.
i don't know anything.

what if human beings are just tiny asteroids?
what if human beings are just tiny volcanoes?

what if life on earth is just a bazillion-charactered play
and mass extinction is a much-needed intermission?

and who am i?
i am littlefishnobody.

*

4

I HAVE A CAT

I had never been a cat person, but when Jen and I moved in together in 2006 after a torrid and turbulent courtship I became stepfather to Ivan and Miss Lucy.

Miss Lucy was a black cat that Jen had adopted from a shelter, and Ivan was a gray cat, possibly a Russian blue, though there's no way to know for certain since he was adopted as well.

"Russian blue" is an exotic and sexy designation a lot of people try to attribute to their cats, but Ivan deserved it. He was beautiful as hell. So much so that we would constantly tell him how beautiful he was. We actually called him "Mister Fantastic," as though a distinguished Russian human name wasn't quite enough.

When we'd see him we'd say, "Mister Fantastic!" as though we were surprised that he showed up in the living room, which was one of only two options for rooms that comprised the prison of his life.

We'd sing songs about Mister Fantastic. When he would dip his head in water, which was the cutest goddamned thing you've ever seen, I'd pull out my guitar and we'd sing, ♪♪ *Mister Fantastic has water on his head! Water on his head, he's got water on his head!* ♪♪

We'd compliment him profusely. "Mister Fantastic! You're so long!"

As if longness in cats were a regal and admired quality.

There's a detail about Ivan and Miss Lucy that's so unbelievable that I'm reluctant to even write it. Before Jen and I moved in together, Ivan and Miss Lucy had spent ten years in the same apartment living like complete strangers. When Jen was in bed, they would cuddle up on either side of her but never on the same side. Jen would always be sandwiched in the middle. Ivan and Miss Lucy never cuddled or had meow conversations or fought or even stared at each other. That always struck us as the strangest choice. Imagine being stuck on Mars with only one other human being and saying, "Look, man, I'm just gonna do my own thing."

But something changed when Jen and I moved in together. Ivan and Miss Lucy fell deeply in love. They cuddled on the couch and purred and licked each other. They shared bowls of Seafood Classic. They became inseparable. So, to this day, though it's corny, we say, "We taught Ivan and Miss Lucy how to love."

When Miss Lucy was maybe ten years old, she passed away after several increasingly grim trips to the vet. She had a variety of old-cat lumps and diseases, and we'd inject her with what we understood to be some combination of chemicals and fluids. They'd help for a few days and then, ultimately, the pain would return. It was tough to tell if the treatment was helping her or torturing her and prolonging the inevitable. Finally, one day, at West Chelsea Veterinary in Manhattan, we decided it would be unfair to keep Miss Lucy alive any longer. We stood by her in an examination room while the vet gave her a lethal injection.

A few months later Ivan started to take ill. He was eighteen years old, which is actually very old for a cat. His stomach couldn't hold food down, so we were switching his food every day. Chicken broth on some days, and on other days we'd liquefy his food in a blender. He needed blood transfusions. And then he would be okay for a while. But there came a time when nothing we were doing was making him feel better.

Jen and I sat down with the "feline quality of life scale" and we both knew in an unspoken way that it was time to let Ivan go.

We hired a veterinarian to come to the house because it felt more humane. At this point, Ivan wasn't really moving and he had parked himself under a desk in our closet-sized office. There were two injections. One to make him subdued and one that went into his organs so that he'd stop breathing. So we crawled under the desk with Ivan and held on to his paw.

It's hard to tell a cat he's not going to be alive anymore if you don't have a strong belief that anything follows this life. So we lay there with Ivan and said, "We're with you, Ivan. It's okay to let go. We're with you. We love you. Thank you for spending your life with us. We will always remember you."

We cried perhaps harder than we had ever cried. Often at funerals there's a sense of restraint based on family dynamics and self-consciousness. But when Ivan died it felt like we cried for all the loved ones we had lost in our lifetimes, all the friends and family members we have lost over the years, and some we worried we would lose too soon. "Thank you for spending your life with us. We will always remember you."

*

& When the cats died of old age...

your eyes gathered light
& grew feline in the wink.

You grew me a beard
for fuzz to pet

       & I said,
"Hey, Beard-o!
I missed you while we were sleeping."

*

After Ivan died I grew a beard so that Jen would have something to pet. Two years later, we adopted Mazzy.

5

I HAVE A JOB

It always seemed that a career and a child could not coexist, a sentiment that has never gone over well with my zombie loved ones.

My brother, Joe, said, "Mike, you can have a kid and a career."

I said, "Yeah, Joe, but it'll be *worse*."

If we're being honest with ourselves, kids hold us back. My best example of this is the history of women...

Stay with me.

I feel like women are smarter than men, and they make, on average, twenty-one cents less on the dollar.

I think women are smarter from birth. Have you ever talked to a two-year-old girl?

A two-year-old girl says things like, "Would you like to have a tea party?" A two-year-old boy smashes a toy truck against his head and says, "Now what?!"

And it doesn't get better. I mean, marginally better. If I were a woman, I'd be furious all the time. I'd walk down the street shouting, "These morons are in charge of anything? How did this happen?"

The answer is: children.

And you might be thinking, *Mike, a lot of people have jobs and kids.*

Well, I'm happy for those imaginary people, but I'd like to bring up two more points:

1. It took me a long time to figure out anything I was good at. I wasn't good at video games or archery or whatever the hell kids do.
2. If I don't take the jobs that come my way, I probably won't get any more jobs. If I pass on taking a gig, I risk the phone not ringing the next time. Not to mention, my job is on the road, and kids need stability. You know what *isn't* stable? *Everything on the road.*

When I was twenty-five, my friend Chris, the person who cast me in my college improv troupe, told me he was thinking of moving back to Chicago from New York City to be a dad and a husband. We had just performed an improv show together after handing out flyers for it all afternoon in Washington Square Park and it had gone pretty well. So when Chris told me he might move, I was shocked.

I said, "Chris, you don't understand. We're gonna make it."

Chris looked around the bar we were sitting in, which was filled with improvisers—a mix of already successful actors as well as aspiring performers, and he said, "I look at these people who have made it and I don't want to have their lives."

I said, "Chris. I'm looking at the same people, and their lives are exciting and fun and meaningful."

And he said, "I'm looking at people who are trying to fill a void."

Chris moved away and became a great dad. And I thought, *What a fucking idiot.*

6

THERE SHOULDN'T BE CHILDREN ANYMORE

I think the current children can finish out their term, but maybe we cut it off there.

Because the earth can't sustain more people. We were given the earth and we failed. I live in New York City, a supposedly liberal city, but, if we're being honest, we barely recycle. We have the garbage and the blue bin, which people basically stuff things into at random and say, "Is this anything? Here's some batteries stuffed in an ink cartridge. Can you turn that into something else?" And then all of that waste is stuffed into trucks and shipped to Pennsylvania, which is fine until New York sinks into the ocean and we all have to move to Pennsylvania. Then we'll all live in homes made of almond milk jugs and laser discs and we'll vacation at Blu-ray mountain.

I'm genuinely perplexed by the environmental crisis and I don't have the answer. Maybe we need to reframe it. Maybe we call it "Save God's Earth" because, according to the book my grandmother gave me for my first communion, God gave us the earth.

He made it in six days...it would have taken thirty if it was a union job. He spent a day on light, which, as a filmmaker, I respect.

On the second day, God created the sky, which is currently overwhelmed with "light pollution"—the brightening of the night sky caused by streetlights and other man-made sources.

On the third day, God created the oceans, the land, and all the plants. He didn't put millions of tons of oil and plastic in the ocean. He thought he'd save some stuff for us to do. And he filled the land with natural resources that we could grow food on and create energy from and then he thought, *There's an outside chance they'll use up all the natural resources and start drilling into the core of the earth, but they probably won't do that because that would poison the water for their children, not to mention the damage it would do to the plants I gave them. Those beautiful, nutrient-filled plants. There's no way they'll genetically alter those plants so that the plants no longer have all these godly nutrients.*

On the fourth day, God created the sun, the moon, and the stars—which feels implausible.

The sun's diameter is 109 times the size of earth's—so that seems like a logistical challenge. That's like if you said, "I'm gonna build a bicycle, a tricycle, and the sun."

On the fifth day, God created the birds, fish, and other sea creatures. *Surely*, God thought, *the populations of these species won't decrease at an unsustainable rate from overfishing. And there's no way people will want more fish than that such that they'll squeeze the eggs out of the fish I made them to create billions more fish in fish farms.*

On the sixth day, God created all the land animals and people. God dreamed that the animals and people would live in harmony and the people would only eat the animals *when necessary* since he already gave them all those plants and fish. I'm sure God thought, *They won't need to slaughter all the animals and keep them in cages the size of their bodies and then force them to eat their own excrement.*

On the seventh day, God rested, which would hopefully set a precedent that people would rest once a week in church-like ceremonies, and the children who lit the candles at the ceremonies would not be systematically molested by men pretending to be super close friends with God. Seriously, they're very close, and don't ask too many questions.

But despite all of these catastrophic possibilities, God believed that if the people he created were brave enough to have faith in the possibility of his unlikely existence, they might also have enough faith in themselves to take care of the gift that he gave them, because if God spent six days creating the earth for these people, the least they could do is spend six days helping God clean up.

But until then—I'm not sure we should be bringing more of God's irresponsible children into God's beautiful earth.

*

Earth (in reverse)

One morning, I decide to spin backwards around the sun, says Earth.
                                    One step behind
                        another behind another, I watch the chipper dance
                        of human beings in reverse.

                        Fork-by-fork,
                I watch these graceful creatures
                pull meat from their mouths
                & plate them & knife them whole.

                        Bucket-loads of tuna
                moving backwards in the fisherman's boat
                remember how to breathe—

                                & the gasping fish
                                spool in
                                to swim on & live their lives.

                & human beings,
                one step behind another behind another,
                are heroes of the earth.

Axes like tree-erecting wands, harpoons like Band-Aids.
        Bombs & guns like surgeons
        extracting shrapnel & mushroom fire.

Such superior intellect, one step behind
another behind another,
walking my soil?

        It always comes back to the soil, says Earth.
        Flybys unpoison the crops
        which unkill the animals
        & untumor the children

        & hospitals release them all—
                        into parking lots.
Moving backwards in their vehicles
they remember
how to breathe.
Swim on & live their lives—

        Inside the mouth-cheeks of human beings
                I see tongues
                word-by-word,
                in reverse:

EARTH as HTRAE and TREE as EERT
when you say it backwards
        Soldiers escorting citizens
        to their rightful homes.

        But human beings, barefoot
one step behind another behind another,
across the bedroom carpet
have their pleasures to pursue—

The unrumpling
of underwear leg-by-leg,
the fingers help it, thigh-high
over the smooth or hairy face
    of the ass.

    This is the only animal that does this, says Earth.

    First with the mouth,
then the hands—
    The cupping, strapping,
    click of fastenings.
The garment-by-garment dressing of the waist & torso.

    The slipping on
    of fabrics— the shirting,
    zippering, the loop-by-loop
    buttoning, belting, skirting.

    The (more mouth)
    smothering of the lips
until both parties are fully clothed
    & embrace for the first time.

    Of perspiration & recollection
    they neaten each other's hair.
    Of fingers-tips. Separate–
        EARTH as HTRAE, TREE as EERT.

*

7

PEOPLE AREN'T GREAT

The conventional wisdom is that people are generally good, but are they?

I'm not sure.

I think women are okay, I think men are on thin ice. Of what I know historically (if you zoom out), and currently (if you zoom back in). And even personally. I mean, think about the men you know. Think about the men you've met in your life. When I do that, I think three or four are horrible. Like, unspeakable. I think the majority are decent.

I think that's sort of the ceiling for men.

I think good is aspirational. I think great is a fantasy. If you're with someone who's great, get outta there.

The men we used to think were great were priests, politicians, and gymnastics doctors. It hasn't ended well for "great."

Sometimes it's hard to tell. When I was twenty-three, I was in Amsterdam with a friend of a friend, which is a cautionary type of person. A friend of a friend is someone you murder people with or who sells you steak knives. We were walking through one of the red-light districts. This is how naive I was at twenty-three: I didn't know what that even meant. If *you* don't know, red-light districts are these neighborhoods in Amsterdam that have, literally, hundreds of prostitutes in windows that are illuminated by red lights. So, we're walking through one of these neighborhoods and I'm thinking these red-light establishments must be bars or maybe strip clubs.

And I said to my friend of a friend, "Should we go in one?"

He said, "Yeah, but we gotta choose carefully."

"How come?"

"It's expensive."

"How expensive?"

"It's about two hundred dollars."

I said, "Two hundred dollars to go into a strip club?!"

He said, "No, they're prostitutes."

I said, "We gotta choose carefully."

I want to be very clear: I don't want to tell you this story. It's the only story I will tell you in this book that I really *don't* want to tell, but I feel like it's essential to the larger story I'm telling…

I chose someone who didn't have a long line.

There was something about the line that made it too real. Like, if I were waiting in a line, I could imagine thinking, *The line for this prostitute is outrageous!*

I chose someone who sort of looked like me. She was a cross between Matt Damon and Bill O'Reilly. She walked me up these rickety steps into this room that was brightly lit and spare— there was only a bed the shape of a gurney. Then she said, "Take off all your clothes and sit on the bed."

And I did that.

And my body was not excited, which is a euphemism.

For my penis.

And, I thought that would be it. I thought she'd call it like an umpire at a baseball game. She'd throw her hands up and shout: "Rain delay!"

But that's not what happened. What happened was she put a condom on…the thing…which I didn't know was physically possible. I grew up in central Massachusetts and we had health class in seventh grade and we put a condom on a banana but never on a water balloon.

She put the thing on the thing and started fellating the thing. And then, if I were to guess, I'd say that about forty seconds later, I concluded the aforementioned activity that I'm uncomfortable describing in detail because of my Catholic upbringing.

And then she said, "I guess you're done."

And I said to her, and I'll never forget this, I said, "Can't we just hang out?"

I'm telling you this long, embarrassing story to make the point that I consider myself...

Decent.

So, I explain all of this to Jen. Because it's part of my larger point. I say, "Clo, why would you want to bring a child into this world with me? I'm miserable, my body's a lemon, I'm a walking preexisting condition, the earth is sinking into the ocean, we're about to be living in the movie *Waterworld*, which did terribly at the box office. People are horrible and I'm not great."

Jen listens to me, then utters in her sweetest, softest, thread-counted voice:

"I know all of that and I think you'd be a good dad."

Then there was a lot of space.

II.

VOWS

I'd be remiss if I chalked up our decision to have a child to *one single moment.*

Nothing ever is.

In movies and plays it's always *a moment* that determines a major life decision, but in life it's more fluid—a series of moments that form an evolution.

Years ago, after a series of hundreds if not thousands of discussions about marriage, Jen and I decided to go to city hall and take our vows. But those weren't the real vows. The real vows took place in our bedroom and on our green/gray couch, where we talked for hours about what we wanted in our lives.

Our informal marriage vows broke down to three basic tenets:

A. We would never hold each other back.
B. I would be allowed to talk about us onstage.
C. Jen could disappear when she felt like it.

Now we were in the same bed and on the same couch talking about having a child and breaking open the aforementioned seven reasons that might present obstacles to maintaining these vows.

Jen said, "A baby wouldn't have to change the way we live our lives." I knew it would. I was willing to go for it. I wanted to be with Jen. I was committed to her. She was committed to us, though neither of us had met the new us.

But we were about to.

*

Just Married

Husband is food. I mean good
or roof. Which husband? Men,
women and snowmen—Where . . .
is my underwear? Husband wakes me
with licking cheeks. I make pillow
of husband's shoulder & husband.

Sousing the dishes topless for husband:
I douse the mugs & bowls with warm
lemon froth & bubble; I sponge
our utensils: spoon, knife & prong,
for food we will eat next Tuesday
& Sunday & Tomorrow; I scrub
& bristle & muscle the pig-headed pans
with sporadic splash & suds to skin;
I rinse & fill & rinse & empty & fill & empty
& fill & empty to the music of water on twice the dishes.

Husband puts his face in a bowl of afternoon
cereal & we sing: Where, where is my underwear?
In the phenomenal
sock project, I watch husband place lone socks
across the kitchen table:
could be inside a pair of pants or suitcase.

In the earth of blankets, I gladden husband by the glow of lamplight
through the sheets. (Where is my underwear?) The sky drools sweetly
to the ear, the purring animals in our bed. Light snore, the seashore at
night.

*

III.

IT'S HAPPENING

RELENTLESS

Jen and I start having sex without a condom, which, if you haven't tried it, by all means give it a chance. Not with my wife, but with your partner.

It's a phenomenal activity. There are videos of it online. But I'm anxious when we're doing it. I say things like, "I'm not sure!" which is not sexy language. That's right up there with "Is the oven on?" or "I'm gonna wear my shirt!"

Sex is the most outrageously dynamic activity because sometimes it's good and sometimes it's bad and sometimes another human being is born afterwards. What other activity has that range of outcomes? Shakespeare called sex "the beast with two backs"—the imagery meaning that a man and a woman in missionary position merge to form the picture of a single beast with two butts, or "backs." I find Shakespeare's language offensive to beasts. Here you are just this beast—minding your own beast business, and then this Hall of Fame playwright comes along and says, "Wouldn't it be funny if you had two assholes?" You're like, "No, it wouldn't. Not to me. Can you just leave me alone? I'm literally a beast."

So Jen and I are creating this beast with two backs, and I'm anxious because I've never had sex without a condom, which is a shocking experience. Having sex without a condom is like going on a road trip and then halfway through the trip, the car just...flies.

You're thinking, *This is better!! There's no traffic and we can go ANYWHERE!!*

That said, I'm anxious during our car-flying sex to the point of pain. I have this embarrassing symptom where I have a pins-and-needles sensation in my urethra the moment I ejaculate.

Which at first is exciting.

I think, *Oh! Maybe this is a new type of orgasm. Maybe I've broken through!*

But then the pain doesn't go away. I think, *Oh no.* It's like when you're eating spicy food and you think, *That's hot. That's hot! That's too hot!!*

But it's with my penis, which is much higher stakes than my tongue.

Dr. Kaplan is not worried. He says, "It's probably just a muscular thing. You're just trying too hard when you're having sex."

I think, *You're telling me.*

He tells me to relax during sex, which has echoes of "Relax your butt," another one of Dr. Kaplan's catchphrases. I've never been good at relaxing. I think somewhere deep inside me I've always thought, *Why would I relax when I'm about to fail? I need to try hard as I fail!* And they definitely didn't have a relaxed attitude when they taught us about sex in Catholic school. In fairness, they didn't teach us about sex. They just implied that we should imagine Jesus crying.

So I try to relax during sex but I still have some trepidation about the whole idea, so the next day I call Joe and I say, "I'm freaking out because I'm flying the car."

Joe says, "What's the worst thing that could happen?"

I say, "I don't think you're following the analogy. I'd have a kid."

He says, "What's the second-worst thing?"

I say, "Two kids."

He says, "That's my life."

I say, "Right." And then I say, "Is there anything I should know?"

Joe says, "You can't know what it's like to have a kid until you have a kid."

"Can you be more specific?"

Joe takes a long, deep breath and says, "It's relentless."

"What do you mean by relentless?"

"You know how you go to the gym and you push and you sweat and it sucks?"

"Yeah."

"When you have a kid, you can't even go to the gym."

Then Joe says, "Look, Mike, I'm not worried about you because whatever happens, whether you have a kid or not, it's not gonna be better or worse. It's just gonna be...new."

FLAT SODA

Jen and I attempt to conceive for eight months, and it doesn't work because my body is a lemon and my boys don't swim.

Which killed me because if I knew that in my twenties, I would have had a much better time. In my twenties I treated my sperm like it was plutonium. I thought, *Don't let that sperm anywhere near those eggs!* Like there'd be an outbreak of these tiny, neurotic Mike Birbiglia toddlers running around the playground saying, "Why would I slide down the slide when I could just walk down the steps?"

Turns out I don't have plutonium. I have flat soda and my boys don't swim. Which isn't surprising because I don't swim. I mean, I occasionally swim, but I prefer to float in circles and I'm always ordering hot dogs at the side of the pool, which is not a quality you want in your sperm, that hungry, lethargic quality.

I discover that my boys don't swim when I go to Dr. Kaplan. He asks me to masturbate into a cup.

I say, "That's rude."

He says, "It's a medical procedure called masturbating into a cup."

I say, "If it's for science, sure."

Two things about masturbating into a cup at the doctor. I'll limit it to two. I could write about this for sixty pages.

1. Everyone knows what's happening—the doctors, the nurses, the people in the waiting room, the UPS guy down the hall.

Meanwhile, you're trying to play it cool, casually whipping off phrases like, "What *I'm* worried about is Brexit!" or "Sea levels sure are rising rapidly!" Everyone's looking at you as if to say, *You're about to ejaculate into Tupperware.*

2. They give you porn—and it's the most extreme porn I've ever seen. I think, *Easy, medical porn.* Here I was all these years thinking that I'm taking in the USDA-recommended level of porn. Turns out that was not enough. Apparently, I needed a "multi."

So Dr. Kaplan calls me a few days later with the results and says, "You're gonna have to come back in and masturbate into a cup again."

And now I'm thinking, *Is this a joke?* Because I'm in the jokes business, and, actually, that would be a pretty good joke where you ask a complete stranger to masturbate into a cup and then, if he falls for it, you'd be like, "He did it!" Everyone would be like, "He did?" You'd be like, "Yeah! Now what do we do?" "Ask him to do it again!" "Ask him to do it again?! Why would he do it again?" "I don't know! I don't know why he did it in the first place! *This whole thing is a sham!*"

A cup, by the way, being the least-conveniently-shaped receptacle one could attempt to masturbate into. A cup assumes a level of composure and accuracy that is frankly rare in this particular activity. A cup assumes the precision of an archer, as though you shoot your sticky arrow and it lands in the cup with a *bing!!*

But it's not like that.

It's more like you shoot your sticky arrow and the arrow breaks apart and some of it gets stuck in the bowstring and some of it is on the floor and you don't know what to do so you bend over and start shoveling the arrow pieces into the cup, screaming, "It's everywhere! Get me some gloves!"

And now everybody knows.

So I go back to the archery lab, I do the thing with the cup again, but this time I wave off the medical porn. I think, *I'm gonna use memory porn 'cause I'm a Christian!*

Dr. Kaplan calls me into the office a few days later with the results and he says, "Mike, you have what's called a 'varicocele,' which is an enlargement of the veins within your testicles. If you wanna get your wife pregnant, I recommend you get what's called a varicocele repair." I had never heard this term. He says, "We make an incision in your abdomen and we go into the vein adjoining your testicle, we squeeze out the excess blood, we patch ya up, and you can't walk for about a week."

I say, "I don't even want to have a kid."

I have to level with him because it's escalating so rapidly. I say, "Dr. Kaplan, I wasn't planning to tell you this, but I don't even wanna have a kid and now you're describing a *Black Mirror* episode and I don't want to be in that one."

Then he says something I never expected anyone to say to me, never mind a medical professional.

He says, "Look, Mike, here's what they don't tell ya: No men want to have kids."

I think, *That's not true. But tell me more.*

He says, "Our wives want us to, we all go along with it. It's the best thing that will ever happen to you. You'll call me and you'll thank me. It's the most joy you'll ever experience."

I walk out of his office in a daze. I nearly wander into traffic and then I turn around and I walk back in and I make an appointment for a varicocele repair. They ask you to sign these extreme forms that I'm pretty sure I didn't read. They could have said, "We may accidentally cut out your balls."

I'd think, *That seems terrible.* Then I'd sign the form. *Do your best... Mike Birbiglia.*

"We may accidentally replace your balls with those Chinese yin and yang balls."

Namaste... Mike Birbiglia.

The night before the scheduled procedure, I make the mistake of going on a surgery message board. A gentleman who had this exact procedure wrote in all caps:

"DO NOT HAVE THIS SURGERY. YOUR PENIS WILL NEVER WORK AGAIN."

So I call Dr. Kaplan in the middle of the night and say, "I was doing some research and this one guy was screaming about how his penis never worked again. Is that one possible outcome?"

Dr. Kaplan says, "Mike, a lot of these people are gettin' this stuff done by amateurs." Which I picture immediately. Some rogue sportsman geared up with outdoor equipment and rubber gloves, shouting, *"I like huntin', I like fishin', I do varicocele repairs out in the garage!"*

But what Dr. Kaplan *doesn't* say is that the scenario of the penis never working again *isn't* a possible outcome—so maybe it *is*. Sometimes doctors speak in fine print. So I'm worried.

At this point Jen doesn't think this surgery is a good idea. I don't think it's a good idea.

I'm sitting on my couch in the middle of the night, thinking, *Jen would be a great mother and I don't want to get in the way of that, so I'll let 'em tinker with my balls for a few hours.*

Well, tinker, they do. The next morning I limp out of outpatient surgery after several hours and for eight days I walk around New York City like a cowboy in snow.

People say, "What happened?"

I say, "Unnecessary ball surgery."

As if that isn't bad enough, I'm booked at Loyola University in Chicago two days later. I would have canceled, but I was booked with Ke$ha and then *she* canceled. And when this massively popular pop star canceled I didn't realize that I would be post-surgery on the day of the show so I had confidently tweeted: "Ke$ha cancels her Loyola-Chicago performance, but Mike Brbgl$a will be there with even more dollar signs in his name."

When I wrote this tweet, I didn't know that I would be icing my testicles before the performance. So I fly to Chicago and, moments before I walk onstage, Joe calls me and says, "Mike, I forgot to tell you that this show has a decency standard. It says that everything you say must be in keeping with the Catholic values of Loyola University and cannot contain anything obscene, indecent, or profane."

And I think, *This is gonna be tricky because what they have just done to my testicles is obscene, indecent, and profane.* So I hang up the phone. I pause for a moment. I want to be decent but I also want to be honest about my physical situation. I'm exhausted. I'm in pain. I don't want to be there. So I hobble onstage and I say, "Hey, everybody, I'm limping because I just had unnecessary ball surgery. But I'm here tonight because *I am not Ke$ha!*"

The show was decent, though perhaps not up to code. But here's the upshot: The varicocele surgery worked.

Now I'm shootin' firebombs. Slingin' rockets in every direction. Laser accuracy. Everyone I'm even shaking hands with is walking away pregnant.

I'm about to find out that one of those people is my wife.

WE GOT A WIN!

It's a humid summer day when I return from Appleton, Wisconsin, and collapse on our beloved green/gray couch.

Jen says, "I'm pregnant."

I jump up and shout, "Yes!" because I have forgotten that I didn't want to have a kid.

That is how dumb my brain is. Even though I didn't want to have a kid, when Jen says she is pregnant, I think, *We got a win! Now what?!*

In that moment I am more excited than Jen. She says, "I'm not gonna be able to celebrate until the baby is born."

I say, "That might take the fun out of it because I've heard that pregnancy can be very long."

Jen is pregnant for about seventy-five months. I'm not sure of the exact amount of time, but it's a long duration. And the pregnancy is brutal.

It's hard for her too.

It's terrifying because it doesn't feel like we have a baby. It feels like we have a gift card for a baby. We have a pile of gift cards in our drawer from Circuit City and Coconuts Records and Tapes, so we aren't optimistic.

The first remarkable fact we learn is that in a woman's first trimester, her hormones double—

Every three days.

That is so much.

It's like my wife is having her period times infinity. To be clear, I'm a big fan of my wife's period. I'm even more sexually attracted to her during her period in a way that she finds hilarious and almost unbelievable. I'm attuned to her period the way she's attuned to my sleepwalking. Jen knows when I might sleepwalk before it even happens. The way older folks feel aches in their bones before a storm, Jen can predict my sleepwalking and I can predict her period.

That said, this is like a period the scope of which I have never witnessed.

You know how on a clear night you can look at the sky and see hundreds of stars and behind those stars hints of other stars and you can imagine an infinite universe of stars and planets and moons? That's how many periods it is.

The first hint of this is when we interview this OB-GYN, which, if you're not familiar, stands for "Open Broken Gooey Yabaganadanayana." She seems thoughtful and knowledgeable and we walk out and Jen says, "She's a fucking monster."

I say, "I totally agree. She's not good at being a doctor."

But that's not enough. She says, "No, she's a fucking monster!"

I shout, "Yeah, she's a fucking monster!!!"

Now I'm screaming at the top of my lungs in broad daylight on the corner of Twenty-Ninth Street and First Avenue about a doctor who I think is pretty good.

Around the time of these doctor visits, Jen writes a series of poems whose main character is a fish:

*

Fish Doctor Play

"FISH tell me your symptoms."

FISH closes her eyes, leans on DOC's hairy chest: "I'm sensitive to light…sound…odor…when I enter a room, I can smell everything that ever took place. As a consequence, I experience nausea 70–90% of the time and although I try, when my body convulses, nothing comes out…

My skin breaks out into sand-dial-shaped hives but when I try to show anyone the marks on my body vanish and no one believes me…

And then there's this hook here in my eye.

But DOC the worst symptom of all…is when I wake in the morning and the symptoms are gone. The pain is the worst when the symptoms are gone."

*

When we get home from the doctor, Jen says, "Will you go to the grocery store and get me some pretzels?"

I say, "Yeah, I'll head over there in a few minutes."

And then what happens…is that Jen starts crying the most I've ever seen her cry in the twelve years we've known each other.

I say, "Clo, what's wrong?"

She says, "I need the pretzels *now*."

So I jog to the store like a snack food superhero and take photos of three types of pretzels, and I text them to her and she writes back, "ALL OF THEM."

I write back, "I saved your best friend's life."

My neighbor spots me photographing the pretzels.

He says, "Mike, what are you doing?"

It's early in the pregnancy so we aren't telling anyone. I say, "This is something I'm into. I have a lot of secrets, Tony."

He says, "When my wife was pregnant she craved pretzels."

I say, "That's irrelevant."

All Jen can eat for a while is pretzels because she has awful morning sickness. But the morning sickness continues into the second trimester, which is more rare. So we're googling "What happens when the morning sickness doesn't stop?"

And the internet basically says, "That isn't a thing."

And we're thinking, *But it's happening.*

The internet is really not the best doctor. It's like if you had a doctor who was on amphetamines. He's like, *I don't know, man. Maybe it's cancer! Maybe it's blood clots! I'm not responsible for this! I'm just data, man! Yo, you ever think about Viagra? Sorry, I was peekin' at your history!*

One night we're sitting on the couch and Jen says, "I found this one site that says 'blow jobs can cure morning sickness'"— which isn't on WebMD, it's just in the comments section.

Heroes aren't always the people you expect. They're not always the first responders or the paramedics.

Sometimes it's a guy with a laptop and a convincing username.

BOMB JOKES

When Jen tells me she's pregnant I'm in the middle of a 112-city tour.

That month I'm in Pittsburgh—then Cleveland—then Ann Arbor, Kalamazoo, Champaign, Indianapolis, Chicago, and then back to New York City for a corporate event honoring the Association of Urologists, a gig I performed *while I was awake*.

As I stuff five pairs of underwear into a backpack I say to Jen, who sits on our green/gray couch: "I have this new joke: My wife is pregnant, which is exciting because I've been meaning to grow into my look."

Jen says, "It would make me uncomfortable if you talked about the pregnancy onstage."

I say, "Got it."

Jen's intense need for privacy is not a put-on. This is real. And I'm torn. Because part of me is literally part of her and she doesn't want me to talk about it. I don't love this because it's, well... breaking one of our vows—that I could always talk about us onstage.

That's okay, I wishfully think. *This will be our onetime exception.*

That said, it's challenging. A solid chunk of my life is spent living and another hearty slice is spent onstage telling jokes about living. For the first time since Jen and I met I am forbidden from talking about our life together. It's off-limits.

I pass through security at LaGuardia Airport. There's a sign that instructs us not to tell "bomb jokes," which is a phrase that never ceases to make me smile because I know that my childhood self would be furious. *No bomb jokes? Why not? Those are the best jokes!* To clarify, when I say "bomb jokes" I don't mean "jokes that bomb," which I'm acquainted with as well, but rather "jokes about bombs." When I would occasionally fly as a kid my brother, Joe, and I would exclusively tell bomb jokes. Bomb jokes are the funniest jokes one can tell when one is nearby a location that might contain bombs. Therein lies the risk and reward of jokes. We joke about things we are most anxious about to defuse the anxiety of the actual threat. We're defusing bombs with jokes about bombs. Or maybe we're just being idiots.

Jen is pregnant, which is its own type of bomb. Something will probably explode, and, if we're lucky, no one will get hurt. The more I think about it, the more I want to tell jokes about it.

I'm sitting on my flight from New York City to Pittsburgh and I pick up the complimentary *USA Today*, everyone's favorite coloring book that sometimes contains words. I'm reading about a man on a flight from Philadelphia to the Dominican Republic who sneezed and then shouted, "I have Ebola."

To clarify—he didn't have Ebola. The outburst was, according to him, "a joke."

All jokes are subjective, but I feel pretty comfortable judging this joke as not a good joke. I'm not even really sure which was the joke part. I suppose the setup was the sneeze and then the punch line was "I have Ebola." After he said, "I have Ebola," he actually also said, "You're all screwed."

Maybe that was the punch line?

Well, regardless of this aspiring comedian's experimental joke structure, the pilot of his aircraft landed immediately and the plane was met with crews of workers in hazmat suits. So it wasn't an ideal comedic debut for "Ebola Man."

What jumped out at me in this story was that Ebola Man's defense was that he was "joking"—which seems to be the modern catchall defense for any outburst of random, despicable

And he said, "You can eat it in the bathroom."

So I walked back to JetBlue's coffin-sized bathroom and cracked into my chicken salad sandwich, experiencing the airplane bathroom's symphony of smells: urine and antiseptic and mayonnaise. Then I'm gagging. Then I'm eating more of the sandwich. Then I'm gagging. Then I'm eating more of the sandwich. And I realized at that moment that I have what is called a "fecal airspace allergy." And it isn't just if I eat feces, it is if the feces are in the air.

After the nut allergy flight I told that story onstage in San Francisco and it definitely got laughs. But I felt conflicted about it because I thought, *Maybe I shouldn't tell jokes about a life-threatening allergy*, but then I also thought, *Jokes have to be about something*. After that show I was signing posters for audience members and this kid came up to me who was about fifteen years old. He asked me if I would sign his EpiPen. He has a nut allergy so he brings the EpiPen with him wherever he goes because if he has an allergic reaction his mom has to spike him in the leg so he doesn't die. So I signed it. And we shared this laugh together, me and this kid who confronts this terrifying reality every day of his life. I was really moved by this experience because I feel like the jokes that touch on the most painful topics can often bring the deepest laughs and the most healing. That's why I try to talk onstage about my greatest sources of pain. I talk about how I jumped out a second-story window in my sleep and how I was nearly killed by a drunk driver and how I had a malignant tumor when I was nineteen. And *those are my best jokes*.

I'm thinking about all of this on my flight to Pittsburgh and jotting down ideas on my JetBlue napkin, and it occurs to me that this will be the topic of my new show. If I'm not allowed to talk about me and Jen, I will talk about the nature of jokes themselves. I call it *Thank God for Jokes*. It's about how jokes have the potential to alienate us from other people but also the possibility to make us closer. I believe that a shared joke, whether with friends or your husband or an audience, is one of the single most uniting experiences one can have. That night I'm talking about this onstage and it occurs to me that sharing a private joke with an audience is so intimate that, in a way, it's like *marrying* the audience. I improvise to that night's crowd: "In a way, it's like *we're* married." Then I take a long pause and say, "I do."

In the process of my writing and performing *Thank God for Jokes*, the world witnessed a tragic incident involving jokes.

Twelve people were killed in France over an offensive cartoon of Mohammed. The satire was not my personal taste, but what struck me was that these were comedy writers who were murdered for their jokes.

One of my friends said, "Can't these people just write jokes that aren't offensive?"

And I said, "I'm not sure that's possible... because all jokes are offensive... to someone."

I start talking about all of this onstage. It leads to this thesis about humor that the world is shrinking and that, despite people's differing jokes and opinions, civility matters. And it's becoming increasingly important to acknowledge this new reality because we can transmit images and essays and jokes thousands of miles across the earth in seconds. So Russia is our neighbor. China is our neighbor. Texas is our neighbor.

But it begs the question: What does it mean to be a decent neighbor?

I think part of it is just listening to people in the context in which they intend their words.

By the time I end the tour I've included elements of the tragedy in France along with the idea that we are all neighbors and that the act of marrying one another with jokes is perhaps healing.

I perform this show in over a hundred cities and marry over 100,000 people. But there's something I miss: my actual wife. Jenny. Clo. J. Hope Stein.

Jen has always worked with me on my shows and my movies. It's something we've always shared. We are each other's first readers. But now she isn't in that headspace. She is neck-deep in becoming a mom. It's the first time since we got married that there is a hint of distance. We aren't spending enough time together on the couch.

THE POO DOESN'T SMELL

We don't tell people Jen is pregnant for months.

This is fine with Jen. If my introverted wife has her way, we won't tell anyone she's pregnant ever. She'll just have the baby and people will think, *I guess they have a baby?* But not telling people things is challenging for me. I stand up at strip malls and state fairs and give long monologues with segues like, "And another thing about me!"

So finally I say, "Clo, we have to tell someone you're pregnant because you can't just show up with a baby because everyone's gonna say, 'Whose baby is that?' And then we'll have to say, 'That's ours. Sorry.'"

The first person we tell is Barack Obama.

We're lucky enough to be in line to take a photo with the president, and I see this as a tremendous opportunity.

I say, "Clo, we should tell the president that you're pregnant."

And Clo says, "Absolutely."

So when we get to the front of the line I say, "Mr. President, this is my wife, Jen. She's newly pregnant. But don't tell anyone."

Which, by the way, is a great trick if you ever meet someone who you know doesn't really care about meeting you: Tell them a secret. If you ever run into Jack Nicholson, you shouldn't say, "What was it like making *Chinatown*?"

You should say something like, "I have a weird thing about kiwi."

Then he'd say, "Wait, what is it?"

Next thing you know you're doing a deep dive with Nicholson on kiwi. But it really is a decent tactic. When we tell the president our pregnancy secret, he says, "Umm...am I the first to know?"

Obama is hooked. Not only that, but he is doing the best Obama impression I have ever seen.

Then Jen says, "Yeah. Do you have any parenting advice?"

Obama says, "Ummm...get some sleep."

And we're laughing but only because he's the president. It isn't that strong comedically but he's, like, your boss times a million.

Then Obama says, "No, actually, I got something. When you bring 'em home, the poo doesn't smell..."

The president says "poo."

The moment he says "poo," I think, *This is the greatest day of my life. I could die right now and I'd be fine with it. Like, if I make a false move and the secret service accidentally shoots me in the head, in those final moments before my body hits the floor, I would shout, "The president said 'poo'! We're alllll...justttt...peeeeople!!"*

The president says, "When you bring 'em home, the poo doesn't smell. It doesn't smell like adult poo. Adult poo..." He stops to think about it. "...smells bad."

Then he looks at me for affirmation.

I say, "Absolutely, Mr. President." Then I think, *Adult poo does indeed smell terrible.* A belief I hold to this day.

Then he says, "When you bring 'em home, the breastfeeding doesn't always work out right away. It can be a little wonky. Don't freak out. And babies crave structure. In their sleeping and their eating. And if it doesn't work out right away, don't freak out."

Then he pauses.

And he thinks about it, and I start to think about how much I'm going to freak out.

Then he says, "That's actually some pretty good advice."

He compliments his own advice.

Then Jen says what I believe to be the funniest thing one could say to the president of the United States.

She says, "If you think of anything else, text us."

CLEAN FORKS

Five months into Jen's pregnancy, we begin nesting.

"Nesting" is a term derived from the process of birds building a nest with their beaks. In the case of human beings, it involves activities like childproofing coffee tables and building a crib. It's a little bit like cleaning up for a houseguest, except this houseguest makes you repeatedly wipe their ass and then doesn't leave for twenty years. Hosting houseguests is not our forte. Also, being houseguests. Also, having a house. Let's just say, we don't have a lot of clean forks. Or spoons. Look, no one really does the dishes in our apartment and that's worked out just fine for the two of us. The dishes in our sink get cleaned on a need-to-use basis. But there are about to be three of us and we realize that roommate number three might want some clean forks.

When Jen is five months pregnant we host some of our zombie friends with kids for breakfast. They casually ask us, "Where do you think you'll give the baby a bath? What you have upstairs might not suffice."

Jen says, "I haven't thought about that yet."

I say, "Maybe the sink?"

Our friend Katie says, "You *could* do the sink."

But judging by her tone Katie doesn't seem convinced. It's like she's saying, "You *could* dry your hair by placing it in a waffle iron." Like she's really not into the idea, and her raised eyebrows seem beyond her control.

I say, "Maybe we could build a bathtub."

Katie nods and says, "That sounds like a better idea."

To be clear, when we initially rented our apartment, we had no plans for children, so our standards for what a bathroom had to be were nothing. It had to have an area where clean water enters and dirty water exits. Thus, our body cleaning device was technically used as a shower, but there was no way it was ever purchased as an item called "shower." It was three walls underneath a spigot of possibly clean and occasionally warm water.

That was fine for us, but it's occurring to us now that this future baby might be a "bath person."

So we start calling phone numbers from those tear sheets on supermarket bulletin boards. Next thing we know, these two guys who for the sake of their anonymity we will call "the bathtub boys" show up at our apartment, rip our bathroom into a thousand pieces, collect a deposit, and then don't return for three weeks.

After the bathtub boys run out of our money at a casino in the Bahamas, they return to our apartment with a bathtub and a drill. That's when the dust storms begin. Did I mention that Jen is allergic to dust? Also, the sound of drills. Jen is coughing and sneezing and the drills don't seem to be providing the kind of therapeutic soundtrack those baby books recommend.

We are nesting.

The bathtub boys say it's gonna be a day. Then they say it's gonna be a week. Then they start making jokes that it might be a year, and those jokes are not funny because we are having a baby in four months. All jokes are offensive to someone, but these jokes are offensive to me.

This is when we start to get scared. After all, as far as we can tell the bathtub boys have no qualifications except the ability to print out an eight-and-a-half-by-eleven flyer and have a phone number.

When they change the time estimates, Jen has no patience for this and yells at me, I assume with the idea that I would relay that yelling to them. Like a game of telephone, but with yelling. It's like "yell-o-phone."

Jen says to me, "The bathtub boys are liars!"

I say, "I know the bathtub boys are liars, but they have the upper hand! They have a bathtub and we have nothing!"

She says, "I can't deal with them because they're liars. I cooked them chicken and veggies in honey sauce and they're lying to me!"

I say, "First of all, do you realize that my whole job is to work with liars? Show business is practically 'Liars Incorporated.' I perform shows sometimes for four hundred people and I walk offstage and the promoter will say, 'There must have been eighty people in there!' and I literally just saw the people! Second of all, we're the ones who told our landlord we were doing 'minor improvements' on the bathroom and then we hired two guys to come over and turn it into a pile of dust. By that logic, we're liars too."

We are nesting. But not with the graceful instincts of birds. It's like we are flying around with the intention of collecting twigs in our beaks to create a soft, safe bed for our offspring, but what we're actually doing is choking on the sticks and also we have no idea how to fly.

Eventually, the bathtub boys finish the bathtub. Then we install a dead bolt on the front door. Then we get the house childproofed by two other folks who come over and charge us $150 for what I believe to be $3.50 worth of foam bumpers. I don't know if the childproofers are liars, but their explanation of why their foam bumpers are superior to other foam bumpers feels a little light on facts.

Our final nesting decision is to install a "landline." If you're not familiar with this term, there are "cell phones" and those are just attached to nothing, no one knows how they work. And then you've got your landline…no one knows how that works, either, but it's attached to a wire, or "line," and so for some reason it feels safer. In end times you're going to want that landline. People are going to be running around screaming that their cell phones don't work, and Jen and I will be home with our landline ordering pizza and reading Dickens.

So we get one.

But we don't give the phone number to anyone. To this day, no one knows the phone number. I couldn't call us. Which means that when someone calls the landline, it's a mistake. One night I am alone, nesting, and the phone rings and I pick it up and say, "Hello?"

The man on the other end says, "Hey."

I say, "Hey." I'm trying to match his energy.

I say, "Who's this?"

He says, "You don't know?"

I say, "No."

He says, "You better get to know."

Now I'm concerned. I walk to the front window and I look outside because I feel like I might be in the opening scene of the film *Scream*.

I say into the landline, "No, really, I don't know."

The caller says, "Uncle Dreesh."

I say, "Uncle Dreesh, I really don't know you."

He says, "Sorry about that, wrong number."

So here we are with a landline and only one person knows our number: Uncle Dreesh.

As Jen and I nest, we check off various boxes in preparation for this future baby. We hire liars to build a bathtub. We install a dead bolt to protect ourselves from liars. We buy foam bumpers from childproofing liars and get a landline in case Uncle Dreesh ever needs to be in touch. Jen keeps reminding me to install the car seat—this is the one item you need in order to take your newborn home from the hospital.

I assure Jen that I have it covered.

I'm lying.

BLEEDING

One night Jen wakes me up in the middle of the night and says, "I'm bleeding. A lot."

We jump in a cab and rush to the hospital. Jen's feeling sick in the car.

She says, "You can talk to me. I just can't talk to you."

I'm not good at consoling people because I'm a cynical person. Jen is too. Maybe "cynical" isn't the right word. We're both some combination of cynical and skeptical. Cynical is: The glass is half empty. Skeptical is more like: Is that even a glass? Is this even water? Whatever it is I spilled it on my computer. Sometimes I tell Jen really dumb jokes to calm her down. I scramble to think of a "joke" joke. My friend Henry had recently taught me this old-fashioned vaudeville joke, so I say: "I'm thinking of going clothes shopping in that state over the bridge..."

I wait for her to respond. Jen says, "New Jersey?"

I say, "New Jerseys, new pants, a whole new wardrobe."

Jen smiles and then she says, "I think she's gone."

I say, "I'm not 100 percent convinced she's gone."

These are not the two people you want in a car on the way to the hospital—one person saying, essentially, "Our baby is dead," and the other saying, "There's a 5 percent chance she's alive."

I'm struggling to come up with something to say. Jen is bleeding and carsick. The driver is veering from lane to lane. As we make what feels like a ninety-degree turn onto exit 7, I say, "If the baby doesn't make it, that's okay too. Because we have each other and I feel lucky to have found you in this vast chaotic world."

We hold hands until the cab pulls up to the hospital. We fill out the forms. We wait.

People are giving birth all around us. We're flashing them approving smiles, like, *Good stuff, y'all! We're gonna wait to find out if this one's alive, but way to go!*

Jen bleeds for ninety minutes before the Open Broken Gooey shows up and explains that Jen's placenta is bleeding.

I say, "Is it gonna be okay?"

The doctor says, "It's gonna bleed more or it's gonna stop bleeding."

I think, *That's what I would say if I were pretending to be a doctor.*

We have a momentary sense of peace but a larger sense of instability.

We feel better but only better than the worst, which is still in the range of bad. We stay several more hours for tests, but each test result seems to conflict with the others.

One test says: "Great baby!"

Another test says: "Is that a baby?"

When Jen goes for these tests, the receptionist asks us to sign these elaborate forms. We don't bother reading the fine print. As far as we know they say "We may accidentally kill your baby!" or "We may take photos of your fetus and put them on fetus fetish sites."

We sign them out of complete resignation to this process, which, at this point, is wildly out of our control.

When we leave the hospital, Jen's doctor says something that I'll never forget.

She says, "The good news is, the baby doesn't know this is happening—*in there.*"

I think, *I wish I was—in there.*

Magic Trick

I bled and bled. I thought of friends who have gone
through much worse and I bled. I thought of women
across the world and in our own country who have no
medical care and bled. I thought of blood and its magic
trick—flowing cell by cell through time without ever
leaving the body. How differently it performs than other
liquids—

                    girl, I whisper
                    to my belly,
            before they tell me she's a girl,

            my body may fail you,
                        (sorry),
            but know this: your life belongs to you
            & our time together

            it has already begun.

                        *

DANGER ZONE

Two nights after our trip to the hospital, Jen attempts to initiate sex.

It's confusing.

I'm not confused that she wants to have sex with me—I've accepted after years of therapy that she's attracted to me. And the blood itself doesn't faze me because, as I've stated, I'm a vampire and Jen's blood is an aphrodisiac. What confuses me is that we *just* had this traumatic physical experience at the hospital, which is ongoing and unresolved, and then, seemingly out of nowhere, she's in the mood for love.

To be clear, I believe pregnant women are our sexiest people. Pregnancy is the hottest multitasking imaginable—having the confidence to think, *I got another person inside me, but, yeah, I'll bang you.*

That said, sex during the pregnancy is hard to predict. Jen doesn't really want to have sex. Or not have sex. Or eat. Or not eat. Or do anything. Or not do anything. Which stands to reason. There's a person inside of her doing the amniotic backstroke and practicing mixed martial arts on her rib cage. That might throw off my rhythms as well.

Jen and I have always had an unspoken communication. We once went to couples therapy and I said, "I feel like you want me to read your mind."

Jen said, "Right."

I said, "Got it."

Over the years I've figured out how to read Jen's mind and now, all of a sudden, there is another mind too. And that's what I don't see coming.

Which is all to say, two nights after we return from an emergency trip to the hospital—I misread the romantic signals.

At 11:00 p.m. I take a shower.

At 11:13 p.m. I exit the shower and walk into the living room, wearing a towel.

Then Jen says, "You're not interested in me"—which is not true.

I say, "That's not true."

She's clearly upset.

I say, "Did you want to have sex?"

She says, "Yes, but forget it now."

I say, "How could I have possibly known?"

She says, "I offered to scrub your back."

I jog my memory. Yes. She had said that. Fuck. I must have thought she meant she'd *scrub my back*.

So here I am. It's 11:20 p.m. I've misread the signals, to my own detriment. I understand she's hurt and insecure, but I can't grasp the idea of begging her to ask me to make a sexual advance when that advance is entirely contingent on her health and not mine. I have no idea what her sexual capacity or interest is and I have no way of knowing—unless she tells me. Which she didn't. Or did. In *back-scrubbing code*.

So now I'm standing in the kitchen, sulking.

Jen sits down on the couch, sulking at me for sulking.

Which is the greatest injustice in relationship dynamics in the history of humankind.

1. Person 1 gets mad at Person 2.
2. Person 2 gets counter-mad at Person 1 for *being mad*.
3. Person 2 apologizes for a thing Person 2 doesn't really even understand and buys Person 1 a pint of ice cream.

So somehow she gets ice cream and an apology, but guess what? *I'm still secretly mad.* I exit the apartment on a mission.

I walk to the grocery store to buy ice cream. No pomp and circumstance. No ice cream photo shoots.

I deliver her a pint of McConnell's cookies and cream with my sweetest, softest-thread-counted voice and I turn on a movie.

Movies have always been a sure thing for me and Jen. They are almost our religion. The film is the gospel. Our discussion afterwards is the homily. The coffee and doughnuts are the coffee and doughnuts.

I will confess that I have, on occasion, lied about my opinion of a movie for the sake of our marriage. I have been known to tell my wife I *love* a movie when in fact I only *like* a movie. I once made the mistake of telling Jen that I only *liked* her favorite film *Picnic at Hanging Rock* and didn't love *Picnic at Hanging Rock*. It nearly ended our marriage. If you're not familiar with *Picnic at Hanging Rock*, it's a 1975 Peter Weir Australian mystery drama hinging on the mystery of: Why is this movie so popular? Seriously, why?

So here I am. It's almost midnight and I need to deliver a movie that is a sure thing. So as Jen sits on the couch, downing a pint of cookies and cream, I turn on what I believe to be one of the most feel-good films of all time: *Top Gun*.

As I press "play," I say to Jen, "I really think you'll love this movie."

Then, as an afterthought, I say, "It's sort of who I am."

Jen says, "It's who you are?"

I say, "It was a big part of my childhood."

One piece of advice: Don't force your partner to watch a film you haven't seen since childhood and don't remember that well and preface it with the phrase "this is who I am."

I had forgotten that *Top Gun* is a homoerotic fighter-jet film. We're watching this scene where the handsome fighter-jet pilots are playing beach volleyball and they're shirtless and oiled up. They don't look a whole lot like me.

And my pregnant wife leans over on our green/gray couch and whispers, "Is this the movie that's *who you are?*"

I try to explain it. I say, "I was eleven years old. I was at John

Casey's birthday party. After the movie ended we all danced to the theme song 'Danger Zone.'" The more I explain, the more I feel myself becoming less sexy in real time.

But by the time the film ends and the Righteous Brothers' "You've Lost That Lovin' Feelin'" reprises, Jen offers to scrub my back.

This time I do not make the same mistake. We had momentarily lost that loving feeling, but now it's back.

Top Gun wins again. Great balls of fire.

Maybe it's the exact level of escapism we need to take our minds off the pregnancy.

Maybe it's the toe-tapping soundtrack that brings back that loving feeling.

Or maybe, just maybe—in that moment—Jen looks within my soul and spots my inner shirtless fighter-jet pilot who merely yearns to blow off steam with a little beach volleyball.

Maybe this is who I am.

DADDYMOON

When Jen is six months pregnant I go on a solo vacation. Not on purpose. That's just how it goes down.

I had planned a "babymoon" up the coast of California. If you're not familiar with the term "babymoon," it's a trip where you take your pregnant wife on a vacation to celebrate that you'll never be alone together ever again. Ever. Again, ever.

Jen and I had gone to the beach on our second date twelve years ago so I could establish that I was a "beach person," and then we never went to the beach again.

That said, I plan this trip up the coast of California and figure out how to pay for it with gigs along the way. So every three days on our "vacation" I have to do a show. That way we don't go broke before spending our savings on diapers, babysitters, and therapy.

Unfortunately, Jen is still bleeding when the babymoon date arrives, so her doctor suggests she not fly because she classifies Jen's pregnancy as "high risk." Obviously, it's a tough pill to swallow when someone cancels on "the last time you're ever going to be alone together for the rest of your lives." Somehow I make my wife's high-risk pregnancy of our unborn child about me. Nevertheless, I booked all these gigs so I have to make the trip alone.

Now it's a daddymoon.

Every night I'm alone in the honeymoon suite of a different

beachside resort, and after the shows I sit alone in a heart-shaped tub eating chocolates and drinking champagne.

So one morning, I find myself sitting poolside on a lounge chair overlooking a beach in Santa Barbara. I'm sitting there without my shirt. On the table next to me is a tube of Banana Boat SPF 50. Somehow I can't muster the energy to put it on. It's always hard to justify applying sunblock because I know that I cannot reach every square inch of my skin, so putting on sunblock becomes amateur body painting. A day after I get heavy sun, my body looks like a red-and-white abstract painting. People look at my back and say, "Is that a cloud? Is that a bunny?"

I have to explain, "That's an area where my arms don't reach." Shit. I have short arms. I hope my kid doesn't get my short arms.

I look across the pool at another couple rubbing sunblock on each other. I think about asking to join their team.

Room for three at this sunblock party?

Probably not the best idea.

If Jen were here I'm not sure I'd even subject *her* to applying my sunblock. It's an involved process. My body has all kinds of dips and grooves. It's like asking someone to butter a walrus.

I'm sitting on the lounger, and a seagull sits on the chair next to me. He's huge. I'm not gonna say he's the size of a person, but it feels like he's the size of a person. It's possible that the Klonopin has not worn off at this point in the morning. So a seagull who seems like he's the size of a person is sitting on a chair next to me eating home fries. Someone has left their half-eaten plate of food from earlier. I'm starting to get worried that the seagull might abruptly leave his breakfast and flap his enormous wings in my face. Or maybe accidentally whack me with one of his enormous talons. *Do seagulls have talons?* As I mentioned, I don't know anything. I get up to shoo the seagull from his chair.

I shout, "Come on! Get out of here!"

I'm shouting at a seagull. Even worse, I'm shouting at a seagull as though the seagull speaks and understands English. There might be a lesson in that. We all ask for things in ways we understand and expect other people to understand, instead of entering their perspective. Maybe I'm doing that with Jen right now. Or maybe I should learn how to speak seagull.

I get up off the lounge chair and walk towards the cliff overlooking the beach. I have a pain in my psoas muscle—that's the one that extends from the lower back to the femur. My brain immediately converts this thought into the worst-case scenario. *Maybe the psoas pain will get worse and, in combination with my aging and tightening ligaments, make me a debilitated old man. I didn't even plan to be old in the first place. Fuck. I wake up tired every day. My moods pivot from manic to sad and in so many ways depend on how much caffeine I'm drinking. Now I'm having a kid. Fuck.*

I walk to the edge of the cliff and there's no obvious way to get down to the beach so I climb backwards down these enormous rocks. The smell of the beach and the precariousness of the rocks transport me to my childhood when my parents would take me to Cape Cod and I'd climb down sand dunes at the national seashore.

I think about how my ten-year-old self didn't even imagine a forty-year-old self.

Perhaps the most baffling thing that occurred in my thirties was that I started living in the oblivion I had not imagined as a child. As a young kid I wanted to be a comedian and a rapper and then, in my twenties, I realized I could actually do one of those things.

In my thirties I realized I hadn't planned to live until my thirties.

That's a strange space to live in.

The great beyond.

It's not outer space but it's close enough. It's *outer time*—which is even scarier because you can't draw a picture of it.

Did people plan to have children when they were children? I guess I knew kids who would play with dolls and pretend that the dolls were their babies but, Jesus, we weren't serious about that, were we?

The end has always felt near. My friend Mitch was dead at thirty-seven. My friend Greg was dead in his forties. Neither of these was from natural causes. I always thought there was a decent chance I would go too. When I started to make a living in my late twenties, Joe encouraged me to start a 401(k) and I thought, *Okay, but who is it for? I'm not going to be old. Maybe he's trying to trick me into saving money for him when he's old. He seems like someone who could be old.*

Aging is like climbing to the top of a mountain and then you either jump off and die or inch your way down until you fall to your death. I never imagined the inching part, just the climbing. Not to mention, if God wanted me to die, sending me through a double-paned window in my sleep at a motel in Walla Walla, Washington, might not be the least obvious sign.

He must have been watching me jump through that window and thinking, *This motherfucker can't do anything right.* I look around at people my age and I think, *Now what do we do? We've peaked. We're like soft avocados. We should have stickers on us that say "ripe ready to eat."*

I arrive at the bottom of the rocks, and my feet hit the beach. The physical act of standing in sand has always shocked me into the present. I walk down the beach, staring out at the waves and the cliffs in the distance.

The beach has always appealed to me. The simple act of walking into the ocean reminds me that I'm alive.

The beach has always been exciting because it's a force larger than myself. I never really believed in God, but I believe in the earth. I believe it is bigger than me. In case you didn't look at the author photo, it is.

I'm standing on the sand and my phone vibrates.

It's Jen.

I pick it up and immediately enter a world of dropped syllables and static. It's amazing how your phone signal can be so clear when it's ringing and then, the moment the connection is made, it drops out like a messenger who travels the world on foot just to say, "There's a message for you."

And then dies.

Jen explains through patches of static that the bleeding has continued and that, to make matters worse, the doctor noticed that Jen has hypermobile hips. The doctor expressed concern that Jen might break or dislocate her hip during labor, which is obviously not great timing.

I say, "Clo, I'm so sorry."

Jen says, "Thanks. How are you doing?"

I say, "Things are fine."

Things aren't fine. I'm away from the person I love most, who is bleeding and anxious about giving birth, and I didn't even want to have a child in the first place.

I say, "I love you. It'll be okay."

We hang up.

I don't know if it'll be okay.

*

A Fish Calls a Human on a Cell Phone

Hello] I'm a—]
]] Hell—

]   I'm a   ]]
a fish.
A FISH.

hell
—
o?

]] damn phone
there is no animal like you]

]] hello
]I'm a

[I'm a
]]
]   ffff   ]hello!

 [damn fffff—
I'm a—[[

Hello.

*

BABY'S EYES

Jen and I are so nervous about her hypermobile hips that we sign up for a holistic birthing education class, which isn't a great fit.

For starters, it involves a lot of class participation, and my beloved introvert isn't eager to share.

The instructor opens the class with the question: "What's the most exciting thing about *having baby?!*"

She looks around the room for answers.

I don't have anything. Jen doesn't either. I'm also thrown when people don't use the word "the." Apparently, they don't say "*the* baby" or "*a* baby."

They just say, "*Baby!*"

We're so nervous that we're thinking, *We just want baby to live! We don't have high hopes for this thing because we went to hospital and we talked to doctor who did test and it's touch and go at moment.*

Apparently our classmates feel differently.

One lady says, "I wanna hold *baby* skin to skin!"

Another lady pronounces, "I just want to see the world through *baby's eyes!*"

I think, *See the world through baby's eyes? How did you make this about you? It's another person and now you've invented this futuristic eye surgery? Get ahold of yourself! What happens if the baby's blind? He feels terrible about himself, like, "My mom only had me for my baby's eyes and they don't even work!"*

After our classmates empty their clichés into the cliché basket, the instructor begins a speech about "the fourth trimester."

"The first few months of baby's life are 'the fourth trimester.'"

I think, *I'm not sure you understand math. You can't just make up new numbers. You can't be like one…two…three…goat cheese.*

Then the instructor says, "When baby comes out they'll try to take her away to check her vitals, but don't let them!"

I think, *I'm pretty sure I'm gonna let 'em! They're called vitals, not optionals! I think we might go with the grain on that one!*

Then she says, "The doctors might tell you that baby's heartbeat is slow, but don't listen to them. This is not a medical event. This is a natural event."

I think, *Um, so is death.*

Jen and I start writing notes to each other with snarky comments, like bad kids in fifth grade. I think, *We should not be having a kid. We are bad kids!*

Everything in birthing class feels wrong. Two hours into the class we take a break and share communal snacks—which also feels wrong, but that's a whole other topic. But this snack break feels like the moment we can discreetly mention the hypermobile hips to our instructor.

We pull her aside and I say, "Jen's doctor says that she has hypermobile hips. We're thinking of considering a C-section so she doesn't break her hip during labor."

The instructor looks at us like a dog being taught math.

To be clear, the C-section is the enemy of natural birth, though it's a one-sided rivalry like the Red Sox and Yankees. The Red Sox hate the Yankees and the Yankees are like, "Right. We're the Yankees." In this case the Yankees are modern medicine and the Red Sox are natural childbirth. (This analogy is offensive to all.)

When we bring up the idea of possibly having a C-section, our birthing instructor doesn't answer. She just gives us this look that says, *Why would you do that? I hope you break your hips.*

*

Fish Doctor Play

DOC cuts into FISH's abdomen.
Her purple-silver scales form a rainbow
under operating lights.

DOC removes a plastic bag from FISH's gut.

"DOC?"

"Yes, FISH?"

"How many hearts is it that beat inside me?"

DOC removes part of a rubber tire,
then a syringe.

"Do you feel pregnant?"

"All my life."

*

To be clear, we're still committed to a relatively natural child-birth. Earlier that week we even hired a doula. Which wasn't the easiest thing to do because we didn't fully understand what a doula does. It was like if you hired a swan wrangler for a wedding. You're basically interviewing someone to not be an asshole and to know more than you do about swans.

We hired Audrey. She seemed friendly and knew more than we did about swans. I privately called her Natural Birth Audrey (NBA). NBA had doula'd (fake word) hundreds of births. That seemed good. And she was very expensive so at least we'd have a reason to complain if she failed. Fear of failure is a recurring theme.

Everything in birthing class feels like something we will fail at. The instructor does a three-hour lecture on breastfeeding: "If baby doesn't latch in the first four days of breastfeeding, don't give up. Don't give her formula. Keep trying."

I think, *We'll probably give up! Is that cool too?*

"If the hospital tries to give you packets of formula on the way out, don't take them!"

Awesome! I think we'll take them. Especially if they're free! By the way, is there anything else that's free?

One night we're walking home from birthing class and Jen starts making out with me because the same hormone that causes hypermobile hips sometimes causes people to crave sex, so when we get home we have this magically pregnant sex with all these contractions and these very loose hips. It's like having sex with Space Mountain.

I say, "Hold on!!"

We're both so afraid that at any moment Jen might give birth into my penis, which they never discussed in birthing class:

No one ever said: "I just want to see *penis* through *baby's eyes!*"

In the third trimester the bleeding stops, which is a huge relief, and the morning sickness goes away but every day contains some combination of relief and pain, sometimes both at once.

One morning Jen wakes up and says, "I didn't sleep all night because the baby's head was pushing into my rib cage and also through the side of my stomach and I couldn't breathe or even really lie down."

I say, "Clo, I'm so sorry you're going through this."

Jen says, "This is the greatest feeling of my life."

SYMPATHETIC EATING

At the start of Jen's pregnancy, I weigh 180 pounds. That's before Jen starts eating for two and I start eating for six.

I'd like to think this is "sympathetic eating."

If you're not familiar with the term, it's when you see the person you love eating a pint of double-chocolate-chip ice cream and you sympathize with them. You think, *I'd like some of that ice cream as well because I'm sympathetic to your ice cream plight.*

Other examples include:

Oh my God, I'm so sorry you're having cramps—are you gonna finish those fries?

Oh no, you're having back pain—we should order Chinese food.

You couldn't sleep all night because of the baby kicks? I like French toast also.

Jen and I have a lot in common. But one thing we've never had in common is food. Jen likes lettuce. Jen likes greens. Jen likes food that is non-artificially green. I like FD&C yellow #5 combined with FD&C blue #1 (green).

Jen enjoys apples. I spend more time with apple derivatives: apple juice, applesauce, apple cider doughnuts. If there's no sugar added, I don't get it. In both ways. I don't understand it and I don't purchase it. Often in the course of our relationship we have divided up one single serving of food. I will order a chicken sandwich with everything on it. I will eat the chicken and the mayonnaise and the bread. Jen will eat the onions and the lettuce and the tomatoes. That is a family meal.

When Jen is pregnant we eat the same food. Cakes and bagels and croissants. One morning we walk to a café and ask for a chocolate croissant and the barista says, "We don't have the chocolate croissant today." As we walk away I say to Jen, "When else would we want the chocolate croissant? If we had twenty-four hours to think about it, we probably wouldn't purchase a candy bar wrapped in bread. We want the chocolate croissant *now*." Jen laughs. We're on the same page. We're bad eaters.

In the third trimester Jen starts eating like a college freshman—hot dogs and ice cream and mayonnaise. One day she's on the couch eating three hot dogs all at once and she looks up at me and says, "I feel like I understand you now."

I say, "I think that's the most offensive thing you've ever said to me. Is that how you have viewed me all these years? Just this ogre who swallows buckets of hot dogs and ice cream and mayonnaise? Sure, that's *a part* of me, but it's not the whole picture."

One day after a trip to Jen's OB-GYN in Manhattan, we make a special trip to Wok 88 and eat a Chinese feast for ten. Spareribs and fried rice and beef with broccoli. We put ourselves into a food coma, though I find that term a little offensive to people in an actual coma.

"How'd you end up in a coma?"

"I was knocked unconscious by an oncoming motorcycle."

"How about you?"

"Rice."

We work up such an appetite sitting in a taxi ride home from Wok 88 that we walk into our apartment and order more food.

When the food shows up we play a game we call "Who Is Less Naked?"

This is a competition to see who is more appropriately dressed to open the door for the food delivery. To be clear, I almost always win this game yet still open the door—making the true loser of the game the food delivery man.

One day we're on the couch and I say, "Have you seen my car keys?"

Jen says, "Cookies? Who has cookies? Do you have cookies?"

I don't have cookies, but I quickly find the car keys so I can drive to the cookies. This is who we are.

Together we eat pizza and pastries and potato chips and potato bread and potato pancakes and regular pancakes and spoonfuls of mayonnaise and peanut butter and double hamburgers and triple hamburgers and triple-chocolate ice cream sandwiches. My sympathy is overwhelming.

Even when I'm alone on the road I go big. One day I land in Chicago for a gig and I order a Lou Malnati's pizza during the taxi ride to my hotel. I lie in bed, eating this platter-sized pizza with a bath towel on my lap.

After I finish the pizza I roll off the bed to jump in the shower before heading to my show. I wander over to the bathroom scale. The needle of the scale springs to the right with a ferocity I have never witnessed. It's the heaviest I've ever been.

I think, *It's fine. I'm pregnant.*

*

Maternity Pants

I always look a little pregnant
        but this is ridiculous.
One part titty-porn/ One part maternity pants.
I have the libido and appetite of a college freshman dude.
Hormone-soup & sleepless,
I misread the word "mega-drought" as "mega-doughnut."
I am a hotdog-eating-vegetarian.
I can feel my belly grow when I walk
        into a home improvement store.
I am a silly result
of blood flow.
When it flows to my uterus:
I am a silly sex.
When it flows to my result
I am a poem.

*

NATURAL HISTORY

One morning Jen and I are lying on the couch and I'm rubbing her shoulders and we're sharing a pint of double-peanut-butter-chocolate-chip ice cream and Jen says, "It's hard for me to breathe or speak or move."

I say, "That really limits your options. That's my big three."

She says, "I feel . . ." She pauses, then takes a long, deep breath. "Like a mammal."

I say, "You are a mammal. We're both mammals. What do you want to *do*?"

Jen says, "I want to go to the Museum of Natural History to be with the other mammals."

So we go to the Museum of Natural History.

We start at the Hall of Human Origins. We stare at the exhibit of humans and chimpanzees who both evolved from hominins. Next in the human chain comes Orrorin then Ardipithecus then Australopithecus then Homo erectus then Homo sapiens. Don't quote me on any of this because "the mystery remains unresolved." But there's something about staring at these fossils that gives me and Jen a sense of peace. We've visited this museum scores of times through years of dating and marriage, but it never gets old. Or, rather, it already is old. It can get *older* but not that much older in relative terms.

We love the museum. There's something calming about staring at dust and thinking, *We will be dust someday as well. Dust isn't so bad! I just hope to get my bones some decent placement at the museum. Hopefully they don't mistake me for Australopithecus. I'm five foot eight and a half and have terrible posture so that kind of mix-up would be understandable.*

We also take solace today in the idea that all of these ancestors gave birth. And lived. And died. And did their best. With much worse health care plans.

We wander over to the Hall of Ocean Life. This is one of Jen's favorite spots. She loves fish. She writes poems about fish. She also enjoys small portions of food as well as swimming. I take photos of Jen with porpoises and walruses and dolphins.

Jen stares at the orca and says, "This is the happiest I've ever felt."

We get to the big blue whale. Jen looks up at this luxury bus–sized creature and then looks at me. She has something big on her mind.

She says, "I know that you didn't want to have a kid and I want you to know that I'm going to work hard so this baby won't change the way we live our lives."

The next morning at 10:04 a.m. our daughter is born.

IV.

MONKEY ARRIVES

A REALITY-BENDING EXPERIENCE

Our daughter's birth is a reality-bending experience because two colossal events occur simultaneously. One is that a human being enters the earth for the first time.

The second is that my wife, this person whom I love and cherish and know better than anyone in the whole world—in front of my eyes—*becomes a mother.*

And I pretty much stay the same.

That's the strangest part because I'm watching this whole thing go down and thinking, *Well, this is nuts. I don't know what I could possibly do to help. I guess I'll just write an email to everyone we've ever met.*

Which is the chief responsibility of the dad. The mom births a living fire hydrant through her vagina, and then the dad knocks out an email to his list. She does the physical and he does the clerical.

I forget to write the email.

I'm not proud of that. It's just that for those first ten hours, I'm stunned by the trippy hospital lights and this chlorine smell, and I'm wearing one of those art school smocks and a shower cap, and at a certain point they hand me this monkey.

And I think, *But we're humans.*

And they give me this look, like, *This is what it is.*

And then you *have to* take it home.

It's completely frowned upon to leave it there. And the nurses try to dress it up. They're like, "We'll put a striped blanket on it and a beanie. We'll make it look like E.T. *You can give it a name!*" So we call our monkey Oona, which means "one," as in, *We're only having one.*

I've been very clear.

In the eleventh hour we decide Jen should get a C-section. The fear of Jen possibly breaking her hip feels overwhelming. We want to be the perfect soldiers for natural everything, but in the final moments we make the judgment call for Jen to not risk breaking her hip.

The quirky by-product of the C-section is that we have already hired Natural Birth Audrey the doula, whose main qualification is that she isn't an asshole and something about swans. NBA's job is to guide us through the wonders of natural childbirth, but then that's not really what this is.

This is literally the opposite of natural childbirth. This is medical childbirth. There are no natural wonders, but there are medical wonders that I am quite impressed by. So NBA sort of stands there as we all witness a non-natural birth.

Jen's C-section takes about twenty minutes. And the doula is usually there for twelve or fifteen or sometimes even forty-eight hours. But I'll tell you something about the doula: If you have a short labor, you don't get a price break. You don't get deep doula discounting. We pay the full natural price. No matter how awestruck we are and how deeply in the moment we feel in this once-in-a-lifetime high of *we just had this baby*, it's still a little awkward when Audrey says, "I think I'm gonna head out."

But this isn't the time to worry about money. This is the time to worry about monkey. We have achieved our goal of getting the monkey out of Jen's body. That said, the monkey is furious. And she isn't wrong. I'd be furious, too, if I came out of the womb. It's just better in there. The womb is like an all-inclusive resort. You're sipping amnio-tinis, floating around in the lazy river. It's soft and wet and warm and everything is taken care of through the cord. The womb is so much better than the earth.

So it stands to reason that when we pull Oona out of the womb, she's miffed.

She's like, *Do not cut the cord!! If you cut that cord I will ruin your life for seventeen years!!*

And that's how it starts.

But Oona is healthy. For that we are so deeply relieved.

Oona has big blue eyes like her dad, a smile like her mom, and miscellaneous other features like monkeys in Africa, India, and Japan. Oona moves and smiles and feels like she did in her mom's belly. She looks exactly like she did in the twenty-five-week scan. Her head is the same shape, her legs curled in the same way. She feels like the same person. As though she wasn't just born, she has only changed locations. Like she just had a really bad flight.

I've never seen Jen so happy in my life. It's almost like I have witnessed fifteen years of my wife's fake smile and now I see the real smile.

And that feels weird.

And beautiful.

And weird.

Just when we're able to have a quiet moment and breathe a sigh of relief—our visitors start to arrive. My introverted wife does not want visitors. In my typical bodyguard role at social events I would explain that *we* had to leave. But at the hospital there is nowhere to go, so I say, "*You're* gonna leave. We're gonna stay here. With the baby." It feels bad to push people towards the exits, but there's a part of me that thinks, *Why do people visit hospitals? It seems unnecessary.* A word of advice about pregnant introverts: They do not want you to visit the hospital unless they explicitly invite you. A second word of advice: Don't ask to be explicitly invited. Explicit invitations from introverts are like shooting stars. They happen or they don't.

In bouncing loved ones out of Jen's hospital room, I have many surreal conversations. Those kinds of conversations where you haven't computed the enormity of what has just taken place but somehow you're expected to say the exact right thing.

One family member says, "You must adore the baby!"

I say, "Yes!" but I think, *It's a monkey.*

Another family member says, "You'll be a great dad."

I say, "Thanks!" and think, *My job is to convince you to leave.*

I'm not immediately in love with our monkey. I'm committed to our monkey. I start trying to figure out how to finance our life with the monkey for the next twenty years. If someone tried to take the monkey, I would have punched that person until they killed me. But I'm not attached to the monkey. I'd like to tell you that I was. Because some people *are.* And some people *aren't.* And the ones who aren't generally don't tell you that they aren't. I would do anything for our baby monkey. But it doesn't mean I understand our baby monkey.

For those first two days, Oona won't sleep unless Jen is holding her. Jen is up all night with Oona but is exhausted and scared that if she falls asleep holding Oona she will drop her. So every hour or so she hands Oona to the nurses to take care of her, but Oona is inconsolable in the nursery and so the nurses bring her back to Jen, which is difficult because Jen has extreme pain from her surgical stitches and is groggy from the painkillers. It's possible that at that moment they both want to be in the womb.

Three days later we bring Oona home. As I've mentioned, the other chief responsibility of the dad in addition to the email blast is to install the car seat. It is literally the only thing a parent has to do to leave the hospital with their own baby. It's the ultimate deal breaker or dealmaker. With a baby and a car seat you are officially a bona fide parent, ready to take your private trainable monkey into this crazy car-filled world.

I forget to bring the car seat.

A toast to the car seat on my bathroom floor

To the car seat on my bathroom floor—
this is how I take my showers—
itsy-bitsy-peek-a-boo with one foot in the air
and the curtain half-drawn—
If the bathroom starts to fly away the baby is secure!

To the lullaby of blue whales and looping rainstorms,
which aid her infant sleep—
She sleeps in no more than 90-minute cycles—
I carry the feeling of being underwater around with me
on a sunny July morning—I tell time
by counting whale songs.

To the backflip she does off the bed—
I move like a character
from *Crouching Tiger, Hidden Dragon* to catch her.
—stick my fingers in her toothless mouth—

Pull out a piece of poop—
No idea how it got there—Her? The cat?
No idea whose poop.

To the scar shaped like a smile at my vaginal hairline
where they pulled her from me—
And the moon-sliver she claws from my cheek-flesh
when I try to put her in a crib —
The girl WILL NOT SLEEP IN A CRIB—

To my poor husband, he would like to go on a date with me, sorry luv, I'm exhausted—

I hold her all night and the scar that is a smile speaks to the scar that is a moon.

A RENEWAL OF VOWS

A day after we bring Oona home from the hospital, I get a call to play a role on a series that might or might not end up on television. It's for a cool network, filmed in New York City, and directed by someone I respect.

That said, Jen just gave birth, and I know that this is the type of quintessential sacrifice that parents make when they have children. It's something I would enjoy, but I say, "I'm not gonna do this."

And I mean it.

Just in case tone isn't clear on the page—despite my many flaws—I am always *very clear*.

I say, "Clo, I'm not gonna do this gig."

Jen says, "I feel strongly that you should do it. This is exactly what we've talked about. We aren't gonna let this change the way we live our lives. We won't hold each other back."

A quick refresher on the informal vows we took over thousands of hours on the couch:

A. We would never hold each other back.
B. I would be allowed to talk about us onstage.
C. Jen could disappear when she felt like it.

We broke Vow B when Jen forbade me from talking about the pregnancy onstage. But that was a mulligan. Everyone gets a mulligan. For nongolfers, that's the extra stroke you allow your-self when you accidentally duff a ball into a lake. Vow B was in the lake. But Vow A is here to stay. We are not going to hold each other back.

I take the gig.

A SLEEPWALKER AND AN INSOMNIAC WALK INTO A BED

When we bring Oona home she won't sleep for a few days.

Then a week.

Then two weeks.

Then a month.

She's the bathtub boys of sleep.

She's vying for the triple crown of sleep deprivation. She won't sleep, she hates to sleep, and she doesn't want us to sleep.

And that's when I remember I didn't want to have a kid.

To be clear, she *sleeps*.

I think they die if they don't sleep, but she doesn't sleep in the time slots we've arranged. There's an expression, "sleep like a baby," which I thought meant "deeply" but apparently means "doesn't."

And sleep isn't exactly our family's strong suit to begin with.

I'm a sleepwalker and Jen is an insomniac—which feels like a variation on "a man walks into a bar."

It's a challenging combination of elements:

Me: sleepwalker, sleep apnea. A fidgety, joint-cracking, mumbly, talking-to-myself, breath-holding, heavy-sighing, tossing and turning and turning and turning and walking and running and breaking whatever's around freak.

Jen: insomniac. Barely sleeps, always writing, always manically thinking. You know how bees have those five eyes and specifically two large *compound eyes* that contain about 6,600 facets that are designed to detect movement? Jen has that with all five senses and can feel and see and hear and touch everything around her acutely at all times. Even when she's asleep.

You can see where this is going.

I've never been on a dating app, but I'm guessing they wouldn't match a medically diagnosed sleepwalker with a severe insomniac. But as Jen once said to me when we were first dating, "You can't choose who you love."

Oona won't sleep and my friend Nick has a lot to say about this.

Nick tells me, "After three weeks their bodies start to settle."

Then Nick tells me, "In six weeks their bodies start to settle."

Then Nick tells me, "In three months their bodies start to settle."

Then I realize, *Oh no. Nick is full of shit and her body is never going to settle. Which makes sense because my body never settled. And Jen's body won't settle. We have a family full of bodies who won't settle. Or sleep!*

A sleepwalker and an insomniac walk into a bed . . . and create a baby whose body won't settle.

When your baby won't sleep, people send you all of this crap.

They say things like, "This is a chair that shakes the baby!" and "This is a blanket that smothers the baby!" and "This is a Magic Sleepsuit!"

That's an actual item. *A. Magic. Sleep. Suit.* You're so desperate for your child to sleep you will believe in magic.

At the risk of telling a "bomb joke," I can only describe what happens as a bomb going off in our living room—a place we formerly knew as a den of peace and solitude. Now it is stuffed with crap. Literally and figuratively.

There is:

The Boppy
The "Brest Friend," which is what I thought I was

Bibs

Binkies

Balls

The toddler rocker

The Rock 'n Play

Ollie the Owl, which is an owl-shaped speaker that tells
you to stop talking

The Moses basket, in case you want to ship your baby
down a river

Slumber Buddies

Dream Dust, which they also sell in Washington Square
Park

The sleep patch, in case your baby won't quit being awake

The baby nasal aspirator—where you suck snot out of your
baby's nose through *your own mouth*. You can re-read
that if it's helpful

Rattles

A rain stick, in case your baby's a shaman

That's about half of it.

And none of it works. Then everyone gives you advice.

"Have you tried sounds of the ocean?"

"Yes, we've tried sounds of the ocean."

"Have you tried massaging her legs?"

"Yes, we've tried massaging her legs."

"She should be sleeping."

"We know she should be sleeping. My wife hasn't slept in weeks . . . though I'm sleeping pretty well."

To be fair, I feel guilty about it, but I have a doctor's note. I have a rare and dangerous sleepwalking disorder. Jen and I are so nervous that we go to my sleep doctor.

I ask my doctor, "Is this dangerous?"

He says, "Oh yeah. There are people with REM sleep behavior disorder who, in rare instances, have dreams that their son is a football and they kick him through the goalposts, which are above the fireplace."

I say, "I wish you hadn't put that image in my brain, but I see your point."

He says, "One thing you might consider is sleeping in a separate bedroom from your wife and daughter and installing a chain lock from the inside."

So we do that. This is our final bit of nesting. I am a dangerous bird who needs a cage. We install a chain lock on my bedroom, and then, to supplement the sleeping bag, I create a fitted sleep sheet that fits me into my mattress. I take a regular fitted sheet and I cut out a hole for my head and one for Jen, though she never used it. And I secure the sheet under the mattress with a rope and a camping clasp. Imagine you're in a psych ward and they have a special sheet to keep dangerous patients in their beds at all times and it only has a single hole for the patient's head so he can breathe.

I made *that*.

So now I'm a relatable Hannibal Lecter. I make this custom sleep sheet, but I need multiples so that I can have one in the wash. I take the prototype of this straitjacket sheet to the tailor on my corner and I say, "Can you make more of these?"

He stares at the sheet and looks perplexed. Then he says, "No."

I say, "But it's a really simple thing. It's a sheet with two holes in it."

He gets out from behind the counter and touches the sign on the wall that says "Shirts" and another sign that says "Pants."

Then he says, "Shirts! Pants!" I believe this final touch is just in case I can't read.

Then he walks me out. Clearly, he thinks it's some sort of S and M sex sheet for Orthodox Jews. Which it is not. It's a homemade medical device.

You might remember we also have a cat. Her name is Mazzy and she was a street cat so she wakes us up every morning by scratching our faces, which, I believe, is a survival instinct *from the streets*. But in a domestic setting that kind of feline violence is much less charming and can be dangerous. You can't have that around an infant, so we lock Mazzy in the bedroom with me. Which means that every morning Mazzy wakes me up by scratching my face, but I can't protect myself because my arms are bound by this weird super-sheet. So now I'm alone in the bedroom shouting, "Outta here, street cat! Nobody wanted you!"

If you have a cat, you know that we also have to keep the litter bin in the locked bedroom, and that first week I forget to scoop the litter and Mazzy pees on this antique linen chair. I don't know if you've smelled cat pee, but it's like if regular pee… took a shit.

Before we had Oona, Jen said, "This baby isn't gonna change the way we live our lives."

And I feel like it has.

Because now I sleep in a straitjacket in a room that's chain-locked from the inside, filled with cat litter dust and super-pee, and every morning I'm awoken by a wild animal trying to murder me in my sleep.

I feel like this baby has changed the way we live our lives.

I don't have a bed.

I wander back and forth from the bed of a baby to the bed of a sleepwalker.

By the time I get to the sleepwalker's bed my shirt is still off my nipples still wet and pointed and wanting to be touched by anyone but a baby when he puts them in his mouth.

When we are done I sleep with the baby.

*

HICCUPTOWN

I'm addicted to working. I work and work and work and then go to sleep, dream about work, have a sleepwalking incident about work, and then roll out of bed and head to work.

As a parent, however, I can't do enough.

I don't do enough that first month. I don't change enough diapers. I'm not around enough. I don't say the right things at the right time. Hindsight is twenty-twenty, but my vision at the time is twenty over a billion. As a parent I am legally blind.

I am quickly demoted to the intern of the family. I run around. I do errands. I say, "Does anyone need coffee? I'll clean up your crap! Someday I hope to be a member of the family!"

I pick up diapers at the natural diapers place. I buy cat food at the natural cat food place. For the first time in my life I shop for my wife's underwear and for some reason I choose thongs. Jen didn't previously own any thongs, but I have never purchased women's underwear so I ask the clerk what she recommends and it's thongs. *Thongs, it is!*

When I bring home three pairs of rainbow-colored thongs, Jen says, "Thank you," but I think she means "Thank you?"

I've made so many jokes about birthing class, but when we bring Oona home I eat my words.

I finally get it: *the fourth trimester*. It *does* make sense.

Jen and Oona are in sync like ballerinas in the New York City

Ballet. And I am the drunk clown who stumbles onstage in the middle of the ballet and trips on his own pee.

Over coffee one day I confide in my friend Nick my deepest fears about not feeling connected and Nick says, "During the first few months it's hard to connect with the baby."

Then I talk to Nick a few months later and he says, "The first six months it's hard to connect with the baby."

A few weeks after that Nick tells me, "The first year it's hard to connect with the baby."

Then I realize Nick is definitely full of shit and that I am screwed. I might never connect with my own baby the way I see other parents connect. I might never connect with my wife in the same way again, and there's nothing I can do about it.

I'm mostly just scared. This monkey in a jumpsuit stares at me with this look like—*I don't know anything. Do you know anything?*

I'm thinking, *I don't know anything either.*

I can't find my role. When we get home from the hospital, I try to give Oona a bath. I had heard she might be a "bath person" and Nick told me a good thing to get involved with is bath time because it's not that hard and it gives your partner a break. When he told me this, I thought, *That sounds perfect! Not too hard!* But when it comes time to do it I freeze up. I'm afraid that I will somehow mess up the bath. I will accidentally drown our daughter. I will squeeze her too tight and she'll slip out of my hands like a bar of soap. Maybe she'll break into soap pieces and go down the drain. We've all read the internet.

Jen doesn't remember me trying to give Oona a bath. It's just another "Who did?" She insists it didn't happen, so either:

A. I tried to give Oona a bath,

or

B. I thought about giving Oona a bath but instead cowered in fear in a linen closet.

I try to change diapers because that's what President Obama recommended. I hear his voice in my head saying, "Don't freak out." But I freak out. Every time I change a diaper I feel like I'm doing it wrong. I think, *I don't even know how to wipe my own ass never mind another person's. No one is winning here. I'm too neurotic to wipe someone's ass. Am I even wiping my own ass correctly? No one taught me this. I've been wingin' it for years. People are gonna see me wiping her ass and they're gonna be like, "That's how you wipe asses? What the hell is wrong with you?"*

Jen becomes so good at being a parent so quickly that it's unnerving. She changes diapers while on the phone and cooking an omelet, which isn't sanitary but it is *impressive.* When I change a diaper it takes fifteen minutes and looks like a papier-mâché sculpture of a broken chair. Jen moves like a ninja—*swipe-wipe-stick-done.* I try to rock Oona to sleep and she screams. Jen holds Oona and soothes her as though her voice is a lullaby.

*

lullaby

little-milk-breath of
morning,
you sip me as day-bread.

you give me no milk-break
milk-drunk of wee-hour,
you little mustache.

little-milk-mouth of cloud-break you suck in the dusk-hour,
you suction the turtle-tide,

little milk-shake of lunch-hour, you little mustache.

you yawn.
dawn.

yawn into milk.

*

I should point out that I'm a decent intern. I work hard. I
show up on time. I follow directions, but I'm relegated to junior-
level activities. Jen puts Oona down for a nap and then she sticks
her in the stroller and says, "Take her for a walk and when she
wakes up, return immediately."

One day I'm pushing sleepy Oona around the neighborhood
when an elderly neighbor shouts, "What's her name?"

I whisper, "Oona."

"What is it?!"

"Oona!"

Oona wakes up and I return her to Mom. As I push screaming

Oona home I make eye contact with a fellow zombie who is also pushing a screaming baby.

We share a look that says, *I think we're doing it wrong.*

Everything I can do Jen can do better.

I start to picture the rest of my life as a full-time intern for my wife with occasional trips to go out and make money for the family. It's the first time I've thought of myself this way. When it was me and Jen I thought, *We'll figure out how to buy food.* When we have Oona I think, *I will buy food and rent and college! This is my purpose!*

I run errands because I know how to do that. I've been an intern before. I know if I mess up, no one will die. And that feels safe. The whole thing makes me realize how much of my life I live in fear. I make decisions out of fear. I dodge obstacles because of fear. The same way I avoided computer science class in college and took extra English classes to puff myself up. The same way I had weaseled out of a middle school track meet by faking an injury. I have dodged everything difficult in my life that didn't come easy to me. But I can't dodge this. It's right in front of me. I can't dodge my own daughter.

All I can think is *How could Jen be so good at this and I be so bad? Does she think I'm bad on purpose or that I was just worthless in every way to begin with?*

I retreat into work. Work is familiar. Work I can do. Maybe that's all I'm good for.

One night Oona has the hiccups. Grown-up hiccups are odd but they're not alarming. Infant hiccups are like if a baby were possessed by the devil. It's like if the devil transformed your baby into a squeaky doll and then squeezed it every twenty seconds. It makes her whole body convulse and make a squawk sound. I've always been good at getting rid of Jen's hiccups. I distract her with something stupid. A story. A song. A dance.

So I pick up my guitar and improvise some lyrics:

♪♪ *"Come on down to hiccuptown to hiccuptown to hiccuptown! Come on down to hiccuptown to hiccuptown we go!!!"* ♪♪

Oona smiles and coos. Her hiccups go away.

The next day Jen hands Oona to me when she's crying. I rock her in my arms.

That doesn't work.

I walk her around the kitchen table.

That doesn't work either.

So I walk her around the table and, as I rock her, I improvise a country ballad:

♪♪ *"I'll walk you around the table… I'll walk you around the table in a circle! And I'll walk you around the table, I'll walk you around the table in a circle!"* ♪♪

Oona calms down. And for those few moments I'm doing something right.

I'm treating it like a gig.

WE WUB YOU

When Oona is seven weeks old I visit my mom at a hospital in Massachusetts.

She's recovering from knee surgery. It's the first time I've seen my mom since Oona was born. When I hear she's in the hospital, I drive straight there and walk in and see the look on my mom's face and I think:

She loves me.

I know that might seem obvious but it's not. My parents rarely told me they loved me as a kid. Instead, they'd say, "Take care." Their affection was akin to a cashier at a museum gift shop after bagging a starfish paperweight. "Take care."

Every once in a while my parents would say a variation on "I love you," but it wouldn't be in a real voice. It would be: "We wub you." It's not the same thing. And, by the way, "we wub you" only came out when things were dire. These were the break-glass-in-case-of-emergency types of situations. This was when I was crying. A lot. Like when my childhood dog Leo got hit by a motorcycle and I could barely speak or breathe. My parents said, "We wub you."

So here I am at the hospital with my mom. I'm thirty-six years old and it's the first time I understand that "I wub you" means "I love you."

I know this because I can see what it looks like when a mother loves a child. I know what it looks like because I spend most of my days interning for Jen, and that's the face Jen makes all the time. It's unmistakable yet indescribable. It's a color not available in the Crayola 64.

I drive the six hours from Massachusetts to Brooklyn. I park the car by the Rite Aid in our neighborhood and grab diapers and cat litter. I walk into our apartment and Jen is on the couch, crying. A lot. Like, pretzels level.

I say, "Clo, what's wrong?"

Jen sobs in her soft, sweet voice, "Oona's never gonna be in my belly again."

A toast to the small gash

> To my doctor casually asking: thinking of having another?
> And myself: suddenly sobbing—
> I don't want to be pregnant with anyone but Oona.
> I don't want to be pregnant with anyone but Oona.

When Jen says, "Oona's never gonna be in my belly again," it melts me. This was the most profound level of love I had ever witnessed and...I was there too.

It's almost like I didn't know what *nothing* meant until I became a dad and then I thought, *Oh, that's what nothing is.* I was so nothing. I was this pudgy milkless vice president of the family. Huge title, no power, also oversees Congress.

Oona is seven weeks old. Jen is a mom. And I am nothing.

DATING MY WIFE

When Oona is two months old we're strolling her through the park and I say to Jen, "I was thinking we should set aside one night a week and get a babysitter."

Jen looks at me as though I suggested we sell Oona into slavery.

Oona starts screaming in my face like the meanest heckler I've ever encountered, like a heckler who hates not only what I'm saying but every word individually in any context. Jen looks at me with a straight face and whispers in her soft, sweet, thread-counted voice, "Oona doesn't like it when we talk."

This baby isn't gonna change the way we live our lives. That said, she doesn't like it when we talk.

In the spirit of "Who did?" I will point out that Jen feels that her delivery of "Oona doesn't like it when we talk" was *not* with a straight face but with a "we're in this together" smile. Jen also pointed out that she didn't look at me as though we were "selling Oona into slavery." She looked at me as though she hadn't slept in seven weeks and could barely see me. She knew that getting a babysitter and going on a date would push her past her point of exhaustion. She was working around the clock and this was the only time she didn't have a baby on her body. This was the only walk she had without pushing a stroller or worrying if the baby was hungry or too hot or needed a change. This was the only moment she could feel a breeze—and I had stolen that time from her by implying that she was failing our marriage.

Meanwhile, in that moment, I feel like I'm talking to someone who has decided that this marriage is over. I don't want that.

I grew up with parents who were married for life, so that's how I viewed marriage. Richer, poorer. Happy, unhappy. These were irrelevant details in the equation of marriage that I had understood. Jen grew up with divorced parents. Jen's sense was that our marriage could end, as sometimes marriages do. I know this now because we've talked about it, but in that moment I *feel it*. I'm a dead man walking.

That day I call Joe for advice.

I say, "What happens when you're not in your family anymore?"

Joe says, "Hang in there. Maybe you should hire a babysitter one night a week. For the marriage."

I say, "Joe, I brought that up today and it didn't go great. When Jen got pregnant we were on the same page that we were gonna hire a nanny or babysitters, but it feels like that might be a little off-limits now."

Joe says, "Has Jen said that?"

I say, "No, but it's sort of in the air."

Joe says, "It's not healthy to repress your feelings."

I say, "Right, but I think it's for the best."

I get off the phone and decide, *I'm going to win back my wife from my daughter.*

I say to Jen, "I think it's important for our marriage that we do something that's just the two of us." I was very clear.

That weekend we get a babysitter.

We plan to see a movie, but Jen can't stomach the idea of leaving Oona with a virtual stranger, so our date is basically walking into the next room and having sex.

I don't remember the exact conversation with the babysitter, but it was something like:

"I think we're gonna stay here."

"So you don't need me?"

"No, we do need you, but we will also be here."

"Where?"

"We'll be in the next room. We'll be back in eleven minutes."

We make it back in six minutes out of respect for her time.

The sex post-Oona is awesome because it feels covert. Like we're getting away with something. But it's also laced with insecurities that are nearly impossible to overcome.

When we leave the babysitter and enter the bedroom, I take Jen's hand and she says, "I look like a monster."

I say, "No, you don't, you look like the most beautiful—"

She interrupts me and says, "MONSTER!!"

I say, "Please let me finish. It's a little unfair for you to alter my sentence midstream. You're so beautiful you'd *scare* monsters because they'd be like, 'We didn't know that level of beauty was possible,' and they'd start comparing their weird monster bodies to yours and then they'd do sort of a group monster-suicide thing because they'd know they could never be as beautiful as you. Also, I'm deeply and animalistically attracted to you and I'd really like to have sex with you."

I've never been great with pickup lines, but that one worked pretty well.

We pay for sex.

We agree that the sex is better when we pay for it.
That we are getting away with something while living
under the oppression of a little tyrant. We pay Anna
Norman from my yoga class 20 US dollars/hour to
hold our baby while we have sex.

I remind him be gentle . . . I remind him be slow . . . with
the pregnancy, birth and breastfeeding everything is
tender and somehow new.

Your ass, he says . . . I'll give him that,
I do a strengthening workout so I can be a stronger
mother.

Gentle, they're sensitive.
I remind him the milk is for her . . .

. . . by the end, neither of us is gentle.
He tells me I am an angel . . . I put my shirt back on
while he is still inside me . . . time is money.

*

MY SIDE OF THE STORY

I want to take a moment to point out that everything you're reading in this book that isn't a poem is my side of the story.

Whenever you hear someone tell a story it's not *the story.*

It's *a* story.

It's a version of the story.

But it's never *the story.*

The best example of this from my life came a few years back when I was asked to host the Gotham Independent Film Awards.

In the audience that night were stars like Claire Danes, Amy Adams, Matt Damon, and David O. Russell.

David O. Russell, despite being one of my favorite directors, infamously shouted at Lily Tomlin many years ago on the set of *I Heart Huckabees.* It was caught on tape and ended up on You-Tube and millions of people saw it.

In case you haven't seen this video, I typed out a transcript of what David O. Russell shouted at Lily Tomlin. So, verbatim, on the set of *I Heart Huckabees,* in the heat of a disagreement, David O. Russell said to Lily Tomlin:

> *I'm just trying to fucking help you, you understand me? I'm just bein' a fuckin' collaborator. I'm just trying to help you fig-ure out the fucking picture. Okay, bitch? I'm not here to be fuckin' yelled at. I didn't work on this fuckin' thing for three fuckin' years to have some fucking cunt yell at me in front of*

the fuckin' crew WHEN I'M TRYING TO FUCKIN' HELP YOU, BITCH!

When I saw this video I thought, *I should talk about that onstage at the Gotham Independent Film Awards.*

Because if comedy is tragedy plus time, this is the funniest thing I've ever seen.

So I was hosting these awards and David O. Russell was in the fourth row.

And so I said, "David O. Russell is here tonight, one of my favorite directors, known for going to extremes to get exactly what he wants. The great director Elia Kazan once said, 'You do whatever it takes to get the shot,' and David O. Russell once said:

> *'I'm just trying to fucking help you, you understand me? I'm just bein' a fuckin' collaborator. I'm just trying to help you figure out the fucking picture. Okay, bitch? I'm not here to be fuckin' yelled at. I didn't work on this fuckin' thing for three fuckin' years to have some fucking cunt yell at me in front of the fuckin' crew when I'm just trying to fuckin' help you, bitch.'"*

Then I said, "Two great directors, basically saying the same thing."

The audience enjoyed it.

David O. Russell left.

Which was unfortunate timing because he was just about to receive the lifetime achievement award.

The woman who booked me for the event came over to our table where I was sitting with Jen and she said, "Mike, David is very upset about your joke. And I think he might leave. Would you talk to him?"

I said, "Absolutely."

Because worst-case scenario, it goes terribly, and best-case scenario, he makes me the lead of his next film.

So I was walking with the event director and she said, "It's my fault, I never should have let you tell that joke. I should have screened your jokes."

And I felt so bad because I wanted to say, "I never would have let you screen my jokes. I would have sent you decoy jokes. I would never hand someone a piece of paper with the word 'cunt' written on it. I wasn't raised that way."

But instead I said, "It's probably your fault? Who knows?"

So we arrived at the men's room and David O. Russell stormed out and bolted for one of the exits.

Then the event director followed him.

And I followed her.

Then David looked back and said, "Give your fucking award to someone else!"

And I thought, *Awesome. This is like we're in that video.*

I returned to my table and Jen said, "What's going on?"

And I said, "Clo, it's a long story and it hasn't ended yet."

Sitting at our table was Jared Leto, but I didn't know it was Jared Leto because he was preparing for his role in *Dallas Buyers Club* so he had lost all this weight and shaved his eyebrows, and he looked like this strange skeleton man. And he leaned over and said, "I haven't eaten in twenty-one days, and that joke made me laugh my ass off."

And I thought, *Thank you, strange man. That means a lot to me because I'm in a lot of trouble right now.*

Amy Adams got up to present the award to David O. Russell...or not. She said, "David is a wonderful collaborator," which was the exact language from the video, though she left out the c-word—which I thought was smart.

After Amy's presentation David did indeed come onstage to receive the award. He gave a wonderful speech. After his speech he sat down at his table and all of these reporters swarmed over to him and they said, "What did you think of Mike Birbiglia's joke?"

He said, "Comedians are gonna make jokes about what they're gonna make jokes about."

Then the same reporters rushed over to my table and said, "What do you think of David's reaction to the joke?"

And I said, "Whatever he said is fine."

That week an article came out in *Variety* magazine about the Gotham Awards and the opening line read:

"Before any winners were announced at Monday's 22nd edition of the Gotham Awards, one thing became clear: Host Mike Birbiglia will not be in David O. Russell's next picture."

And I think that's fair. Because if David O. Russell were given space in this book to respond, he'd probably write something like, "I was invited to that event to be honored by my peers and then this comedian, whom I've never heard of, walked onstage and recited verbatim the most regrettable three minutes of my life and everyone laughed." And that's not wrong.

That's his side of the story.

*

My Side of the Story

Dear Oona, If in a conversation with your significant other about the future—

Believe them if they say they don't want to take care of a baby. If in a conversation about the future, you respond by saying that you have no intention of changing your life, wait to meet your child before you laugh at other parents while promising to be nothing like them. Saying, *It's not good for the kid or the parent to act that way.* Before your child is born, you might say things like, *It's the baby who will have to learn to integrate into my life not the other way around.* Next thing you know you are walking down the street, your baby in a stroller crying, her father trying to talk to you about his day and you stop him to say, *She doesn't like it when we talk*—and you walk ten blocks in silence. Wait, you could find yourself alone in a hospital bed in the middle of the night, the father away on business because you insisted nothing change once the baby is born—and you, at the hospital in the middle of the night, unslept, on painkillers—but holy shit the pain—unable to stand, your baby one day old, left in a bassinet across the room by nurses saying she is inconsolable in the nursery, you cannot stand, she cries out, you stand, you sway you sing you feed, no matter your fresh stitches, she stops crying when you hold her, holy shit the pain, you do not let her go until morning, you wait it happens in a moment.

*

V.

PRETENDING

As a child I felt like I lived in this town where everyone was pretending to be happy and pretending to be in a good marriage and pretending they had a nice house with a nice living room. I thought, *I need to get out of here.*

So I went to college as far away as I could think of. Washington, DC. Everyone at college was pretending to have a lot of friends. And pretending to be smart. And pretending to be well read. And pretending to have a plan for the future. So I moved to New York City. And I met all these comedians who were pretending to be confident and pretending to be successful. Now my wife and I have a daughter and we live in a neighborhood full of parents who are pretending to love their lives and pretending to have nice apartments and pretending to have nice living rooms. Our daughter loves dressing up as a fairy and a princess and a bunny. It's practically the first thing we teach her. To pretend.

When Oona is several weeks old I'm strolling her around the neighborhood. Part of the stroll is spent dodging potholes and cracks in the sidewalk and the other part is spent staring at these zombie parents who I am convinced are pretending to experience joy.

I may be wrong.

This is just how I experience it. One strange twist of having a child is that people expect you to experience joy. One day our neighbor spots me strolling Oona and says, "Is it the most joy you've ever experienced?"

The most joy? Um…I don't know. Maybe?

I don't say this, of course. I think it. I feel like saying a lot, actually. I feel like saying, *I didn't experience joy before. I don't have to start now. Don't impose your unrealistic expectations on me. I will be a good dad. A decent dad. The #1 dad in America, according to several ceramic mugs. But my dad did a decent job and he didn't experience joy.*

And don't get me wrong, I experience joy but it's also a little lonesome, because my wife and child adore each other and I'm perhaps even more lonely because not only am I lonely but I'm not allowed to say I'm lonely. I have to say, "I'm the luckiest man in the world."

My stiff and fake grin creates the expression of a serial killer. My hair juts in five directions, my face is unshaven, my back aches, my shirt buttons are in the wrong holes. *I'm the luckiest man in the world.*

Having a child is like being a pro ballplayer where a young recruit gets called up from Triple-A and you realize you're gonna get bumped out of the lineup. But in this case you're bumped out of… being alive. And after you get bumped people say, "Is it the most joy you've ever experienced?" Becoming a dad is like if you died and nobody cared and people showed up to the funeral for the food.

So I experience joy, but I'm starting to understand joy in a new way. There are different types of joy. There's "light joy" and "dark joy."

Light joy is eating watermelon in the summertime. Dark joy is smoking pot through a watermelon.

Light joy is when a puppy licks your face. Dark joy is when a lady at a bar licks your face.

Light joy is flying a kite at the beach. Dark joy is having sex on a broken kite.

Light joy is watching YouTube videos of cats. Dark joy is watching waterslide accidents.

When I was single I had a lot of dark joy. Dark joy is abundant in your twenties when you don't care what happens in your life. Dark joy occurs when people tell you "life is sacred" and you think, *Nah, fuck that. I'm gonna eat nineteen pounds of chocolate and roll the dice. I'm gonna stay out 'til 5:00 a.m. and get advice from a guy wearing a snake.*

So that's gone. Which is probably for the best because with dark joy, when the joy goes away you're literally in the dark.

When you have a kid you can no longer watch yourself living. There's just not enough time. And some parents try to do it. They pull out their phones when anything remotely exciting happens:

"Mabel just pointed at her teeth!!! Do it again, Mabel! Rolling...and action. Say the thing about your fucking teeth, Mabel!! Oh great, we missed it. This whole shoot's been a fucking waste!"

I'm strolling Oona through the neighborhood when it occurs to me:

Maybe having a kid is the darkest joy of all.

Because the stakes are so high. Your child could grow up and cure cancer or solve climate change, but she could also become an addict or a runaway or have a life-threatening disease. There is literally no way you could know. That is some dark stuff.

It's possible that the only way to cope with these dark possibilities is to pretend.

*

Confetti

I wake to a town populated by fairies and sea creatures and dinosaurs, and my daughter is brushing her hair with a seashell—Several fairy offerings lay on my pillow—a teacup, a mushroom, a drawing of the sky—there are monkeys and glitter in the sky—And I am decorated—with orca whales and narwhals and homemade-confetti which slide off me when I stretch or fidget. And all the dolls of the room are cared for—lined up and tucked under a blanket—*shhh*—*all my babies are sleeping.*

*

VI.

MONKEY WON'T SLEEP

THERE'S NO ME IN WE

Five months into Oona's life, Jen and I are both living our dreams come true, but for the first time in our marriage they are different dreams. I'm on tour with a new show and Jen is a mom. I'm rooting for her and she's rooting for me, but we're growing apart.

One night I'm doing a show in Weatherford, Oklahoma, which is a direct flight from nowhere, which is why I flew into Dallas.

Google Maps told me Dallas was a four-hour drive to Weatherford, but I'll tell you something about Google Maps:

Google Maps is a fucking liar.

Google Maps is like that uncle you have who isn't *going* on the trip but has very strong opinions about the trip.

Uncle Googlemaps is like, "Ehhhh, it's, like, four hours."

"But, Uncle Googlemaps, a lot of these are side roads and that road just looks like a field."

"Eh, four and a half. Don't forget to stop at Waffle House. Best waffles!"

It's a seven-hour drive.

I drive with a comic friend named Mike MacRae and we're seven hours into this trip and he's chain-smoking out the window, which killed me because I had rented the car and I had just signed a form that said something like, "If you smoke, we will take your brain out of your skull."

And I'm signing it, thinking *Mike Birbiglia... I'm sure that'll be fine.*

But MacRae is very intimidating so I don't wanna bring it up. I say, "Hey, maybe don't... I think they might... take my brain outta my..."

MacRae cuts me off: "I've been smoking in rentals for seventeen years."

Fair enough. Smoke away. Don't mind me. I'm just lightheaded and have no idea where we are.

Which is true. After six and a half hours of driving we're running out of gas through fields of nothing. I mean... *NOTHING.* There are parts of Oklahoma where they don't even have molecules. You're driving on a road and then all of a sudden you think, *We're nowhere in space or time... but there are two senators!* Which is *odd*, but that's not the point.

I don't know what to do and so I drive faster to avoid the suspense of running out of gas. The next town we arrive in is literally called Corn.

And I think, *Now God is just fucking with us.*

I'm like, "Uncle Googlemaps, you ever heard of Corn?"

He's like, "Corn? OK!"

Which is just the state abbreviation for Oklahoma. But it *isn't* okay because they don't have gas in Corn. They might have ethanol, but we don't need ethanol.

We finally roll into Weatherford on fumes and, twenty minutes later, we're performing in a giant gymnasium and pretty much no one is there, which makes sense because very few people live in Weatherford, Oklahoma.

All things considered, the show goes fine. When I'm in Oklahoma I just make fun of Texas and when I'm in Texas I make fun of Oklahoma. I say things like, "Those gun-totin' one-tooth idiots in Texas..." And they go nuts.

Oklahomans don't see the irony, which is that they're basically part of the same state separated by an arbitrary border. They're like, "Our state's shaped like a whistle!"

After the show I check into my one-and-a-half-star hotel in

Weatherford. It's 11:00 p.m. and they've given away my first-floor room since we got there so late. I stay in first-floor rooms when I travel in case I, ya know…jump out the window in my sleep.

I walk into my second-story room. A lot of red flags: an old dirty comforter that seems to have not been cleaned in a decade, a mildewy bathroom, smoky curtains, rickety windows.

I think, *I guess I might die.*

But there's nothing I can do about it. I've flown five hours, driven seven hours, and then performed for ninety minutes. I have no energy and this feels like déjà vu with my incident in Walla Walla. So I barricade the window with an enormous standing dresser. It's about one hundred pounds and I push it across the room and block the window and I get in my sleeping bag.

The next morning I wake up and I drive all the way back to Dallas to catch my flight but there are delays from storms. So, finally, after a day of travel, I walk into our apartment at one in the morning and I'm soaking wet and exhausted and entirely empty and I arrive at my beloved couch and…

Oona is asleep on the couch.

I whisper to Jen: "Clo, it's not a big deal, but that's my couch."

Jen says, "Great news. That's where Oona likes to sleep."

I say, "I totally get it and in the short term that makes a ton of sense, but long term I think maybe she might want to sleep in a crib."

Jen says, "We decided Oona doesn't like to sleep in a crib."

I say, "Who's in 'we'?"

Jen says, "Me and Oona."

I say, "I'm not in 'we' anymore? I'm a founding member of 'we.'"

I walk into the bedroom and get into my straitjacket. It is a shocking revelation when you discover you've been evicted from your own life.

FRIENDLY ADVICE FROM OTHER PARENTS

Your daughter is getting a sunburn.
   You're getting a sunburn.
   We're all getting a sunburn.
   Let them cry.
   Don't let them cry.
   I'm great with kids.
   It seems like you're not great with kids.
   Kids will murder each other if you let them.
   You have to let kids murder each other.
   Murder is wrong.
   Murder isn't always wrong.
   Meat is murder.
   The murder burger at this restaurant is phenomenal.
   Get your kid signed up for camp!
   There was a murder at that camp.
   Our children should be friends.
   I have no friends.
   I need you to be my friend.
   Jokes are funny. I like jokes. I am funny. I am jokes.
   Swimming pools are essential.
   Swimming pools are disgusting.
   I'm disgusting. Will you watch my son?

You gotta crack an egg to make an omelet.

Don't let them touch eggs.

Kids love mustard.

Kids hate mustard.

My son is made of mustard.

Why isn't she sleeping?

Tell her to sleep!

I think I just woke her up.

She probably needed to wake up.

Oprah doesn't sleep.

You can't let them walk all over you.

If they walk on your back it feels like a massage.

Here's a book about how to be a better parent.

You need this book.

I haven't read it. I basically wrote it.

My son could read when he was two months old.

Our daughter is better at swimming than yours but she's also smarter.

Our son only edits in Final Cut.

Our daughter's first steps were out of her mother's vagina.

Why don't you give her chocolate?

I love chocolate.

If that was my baby I'd give her chocolate.

I'd like to dip your baby in chocolate.

Chocolate-dipped babies are a delicacy in some cultures.

You need to let her make decisions for herself.

Yes, it is *her* body but it is *my* chocolate.

Where is her sunhat?

Where is my social security card?

Where is her jacket?

She shouldn't be outside in this weather.

She shouldn't be inside in this weather.

The government controls the weather.

My children won't let me near their children so it's nice talking to you.

What's her name?
That's not a name.
Give her a different name.
Cut her hair.
Don't you dare cut that hair!
Sell her hair.
Donate her hair.
Our son hits.
They all hit.
I know our son is hitting your daughter but it's fine.
You need to have a thicker skin.
Where are you going?

A toast to the third arm

To the stranger who offers to hold a door for me—
No need, I walk backwards into doors to inspire a third arm.

To the stranger who hands me napkins,
I guess I look like I could use a napkin.

To the stranger yelling across restaurant tables—
how's the baby sleeping?—She doesn't—
I play whale songs all night to aid her infant sleep.

To the two strangers who scold me—
where's the baby's sunhat!
—as I walk down my own street—
I am like Johannes Kepler tracking the angle of sun
using the planet of my body to shade her.

To the stranger who follows me down the street
as I hold an 18-pound car seat, a 10-pound diaper bag

and a 17-pound baby—
then yells as I decline his help—
You women want to do everything yourself!—

He comes closer—I decline his help again.
He comes closer. I decline—
You women want to do everything yourself—

He is yelling at me—I accidentally hit my daughter's tiny
head into a cab door.
—He is too close to the cab—the baby is screaming—
I am holding her. I am tangled up
in an 18-pound car seat and 10-pound diaper bag—

He is almost in the cab—
I don't have a hand to close the door—
He comes closer and I
FFFV–

He is almost in the—and I—
FFFHUDHUDHUD—FFFFVVVVFVDFVDFVDVUUDHD
HHDRVRHUH—
That's "get the fuck away from my baby" in whale song.
And I slam the cab door.

To the guy drinking on an East Village street-corner yelling,
God bless the baby as I pass—
Thanks, guy.

To my dear neglected husband—he would like to go on a date
with me, last night was kind of rough, luv—

To get this look: sleep deprivation and spit-up in the hair.

*

SEX MAYBE

When Oona is six months old, Jen and I go out for the night and eat pizza and drink wine and reminisce about the day we first met.

Our marriage was as unlikely as our having a child. When we met, neither of us wanted to be in a relationship at all. We treated the relationship like it was a joke.

It started in St. Louis.

My friend Andy and I were performing for Jen's company there. Andy introduced us in the lobby of our hotel, which intersected with a staircase of a mall. So we sort of met at the mall. Well, we met on a mall staircase. It was very American.

From the moment I met Jen, I knew I wanted to sleep with her at least once.

Stay with me.

I had just come off a long, difficult breakup with my college sweetheart Abbie. We were planning to get married and then we weren't and when we weren't I was so heartbroken I just entirely swore off the idea of marriage or even living with someone.

But I really wanted to sleep with Jen.

I didn't think it was going to happen. I've never had that kind of confidence. I think of myself as a "sex maybe"—which is to say that if I'm seeing a woman, she'd think, *I could imagine having sex with him…maybe.* I'm not ashamed of that. There were periods of my life where I was a "sex never" or a "sex with self always." And often. Surprisingly often.

I don't remember what Jen and I talked about on the mall staircase, but I remember that Jen's eyes told a story that was so deep and profound that I just wanted to get inside her eyes and stay awhile. Maybe buy a place. At the very least I wanted to rent.

I asked Andy to convince Jen to go out that night for St. Patrick's Day. We were going to this famous Irish pub called McGurk's and it took so much coaxing to convince Jen to come out that by the time she did, she thought she was on a date with *him*. So I had to sort of push him out of the bar so that I could spend time with her, and then she realized she was on a date with *me*.

She wasn't thrilled about that.

The joke I kept telling that night was that Jen had ruined "a perfectly good night that I was going to spend alone with my friend Andy." This is a classic fourth-grade technique when you have a crush on someone: act like they are in some way ruining your life. She wasn't as excited about me as I was about her until the end of the night when we shared a ride home and we were stuffed in the back seat of this little car and we started talking about the Ionesco play *Rhinoceros*. I was reading it at the time and she had read it a few years before. It's a classic absurdist play and little did we know that we in fact were two absurd people with absurd idiosyncrasies who would even have annoyed Ionesco. When we got back to the hotel I walked Jen to the elevator and I leaned in to kiss her and she said, "Oh, no thank you."

Which was polite, but disappointing.

When I got back to my room, I called her phone. We talked for hours. I don't even remember how long. It's possible that conversation has continued until this very day.

Jen offered to see me in New York, which is where we both lived. She gave me her number and I typed it in my phone and from that point on she would be:

"Jen—Irish Pub—Nice."

When we got back to New York, I offered to take Jen out to a restaurant I couldn't afford so that I could show her how much money I could put on my credit card. At dinner she said, "Everyone hates me at work."

I said, "Why would they hate you? I love you."

She said, "You *love* me?"

I said, "I mean...you *seem cool*."

I didn't want to show her all my cards. Just nine of them.

Two weeks into dating I asked Jen if she wanted to go on a trip to Bermuda. I felt the need to overcompensate for the fact that she was way out of my league. So I invited her on a trip to Bermuda. In retrospect I meant to say Aruba. Which would've been a lot nicer. Because it was the winter. And when it's winter in New York it is also winter in Bermuda.

So we went to Bermuda in our third week of dating. When we got on the plane the flight attendant brought us champagne and said, "Congratulations on your honeymoon."

I said, "Oh, no thank you. We're not on a honeymoon."

When she left, Jen and I started talking about marriage.

I said, "It just seems like a doomed idea. Fifty percent of marriages end in divorce. But that's just first marriages. Second marriages: 67 percent. Third marriages: 74 percent. That's a learning curve. Second of all, I'm never gonna be happy, why would anyone want to be a part of that?"

Jen said, "That's a very detailed argument."

I said, "I've thought about it a lot."

Jen said, "I don't think I'll ever get married either."

I said, "How come?"

She said, "The person I wanted to marry is dead."

She told me about her high school sweetheart Brian. He was her first love and he died from leukemia.

I said, "Do you ever talk to people about that?"

She said, "No."

I said, "Well, you can talk to me."

After we got back from Bermuda, I kept coming up with excuses for me and Jen to spend every minute together. I was doing shows in Ireland and so I invited her to come. We went to Dublin, Galway, and Dingle.

At this point she had completely checked out at work. They would call her from the office and say, "Where are you?"

And she would say, "I'm in Ireland."

One night we were in a pub in Dingle and Jen said to me, "There are special berries from here. I've heard of this."

I said, "I don't think that's right. I think 'dingleberries' is an expression that refers to something else."

She said, "No, I'm sure of it. Just ask someone."

So I said to the bartender, "Is this town known for its berries?"

And the bartender told everyone at the bar. And the entire bar was laughing.

And we were laughing.

For about three more years. Until finally we went to city hall and got married.

And then the joke became real. Even when we got married, no one we knew got us a present because they thought it was a joke.

After we went to city hall, Jen called her mom and her stepfather, Bob, and said, "Mike and I got married today."

Bob said, "That's great, did your cats get married too?"

Jen said, "It's funny you should mention that, because we actually looked up whether you can marry your cats, and you can technically marry your cats through certain websites but they can't marry each other."

We hung up the phone, and Bob called back a few hours later and said, "I'm so sorry, I thought you were joking when you said you got married. I didn't know it was real. Congratulations!"

But it is real. Our marriage is the most real thing I've ever been a part of, but at this moment I feel like it's fading.

I'm sitting with Jen at this small brick-oven pizzeria on our anniversary, and I decide I'm going to tell her this. I'm going to let her know that I miss our old life and I want it back.

But before I can gather the words, Jen says, "I'm sorry. I promised things wouldn't change and they have. And I don't know what to do about it."

I say, "There are times lately when I've felt like you've abandoned me."

Jen says, "That was part C of the vows. That I could disappear."

I say, "I get it. I totally understand why everything changed."

But secretly I think, *I still want our old life back.*

GREAT JOB

When Oona is seven months old she starts to talk.

Jen says, "Hi!"

Oona says, "*Hi.*"

And I say, "Hi!"

Oona blinks. She's not giving me "hi" yet. I haven't earned it.

When Oona is eight months old I find this:

An Infant Reaches

An infant reaches for something (I don't know what)
—pushes it farther away and cries in frustration each
time she reaches without realizing she is crawling for
the first time.

She is like her father.

That's a poetry burn.

That week Oona is teething. As far as we can tell she's growing 237 teeth. The only time she'll stop screaming is when she's
suckling Jen's boob with her freaky shark teeth. Breastfeeding is

the greatest magic trick in the history of humankind. I couldn't invent a better trick with my imagination. I could say, "I can blow out candles with my penis," and someone could simply reply, "That's nice, but what Rhonda can do is feed a child for three years without going to the grocery store." I'd think, *I shouldn't have mentioned my candles trick.* One morning Jen and Oona are at the kitchen table. Their love is palpable. Their existence as a single unit is undeniable. Oona's sucking all the life and food and energy out of Jen, which is what *I* want to do, but I can't because I'm doing the dishes.

Jen says, "You're doing a great job."

And I say, "Thanks. Sometimes I'm not sure."

She says, "Not you."

TRYING

*

a puddle

a toddler dances naked in the window
with a gob of summer squash in her hair.
then slips in a puddle of her own urine.

*

I'm sitting in the living room, watching our eight-month-old
daughter try to pull herself up on the ottoman.
Then she falls.
Then she pulls herself up.
She's trying.
I'm thirty-seven years old and it's just occurring to me that
my entire life is defined by trying. I tried to crawl, then I tried to
walk, then I tried to be Larry Bird, then I tried to get into college, and then I tried to be a comedian.
You don't choose what you remember in life, but for some reason I remember all the times I tried.
When I was a sophomore in high school I joined the wrestling team because my brother told me "it builds character." I
thought, *Well, sure, I'll do it—if it builds character.*

I had no idea what that meant.

I also had no idea that wrestling practice is not like soccer practice where you can sort of blend in. You have to *wrestle*. Or, in my case, be wrestled upon by these young, muscly gentlemen whose crotches would inevitably be pressed up against my face as if they were doing a victory dance. All the while I'm wearing an ill-fitting women's bathing suit. But I was building character and that character was a lifeguard from the 1940s.

In practice we would wrestle and do push-ups, which has never been one of my strong suits. At a certain point in life I lost the will to *push up*. I'd get into that first, facedown position and think, *This is a nice, new lying position*. Then I'd lean my head into my hands and take a break. I'd think, *These are soft, comfy hands. These are nature's pillows!*

I was in the 152-pound weight class, but because I was so terrible at it, Coach Shann paired me up with our 102-pound wrestler. I don't know if you've ever seen a 102-pound person before. Most of them are fat babies. They compete at fairs across the country with dreams of gracing a quarter page in the *Guinness Book of World Records*. This was no fat baby. This was a young, strong high school junior who would pin me countless times every day.

It was like watching a paperweight be pinned by paper.

I wouldn't compete with the wrestling team but I would travel with them. And I would wear the same outfit so that in case there was some kind of brawl, the other team could identify me as low-hanging fruit.

After the competition, time permitting, they would send us B teamers out to compete against their B teamers. And I developed a strategy where I would be pinned as quickly as possible so this portion of my life would be over.

This strategy ran into a snag when I encountered an opponent who had the same strategy. So we're both out there treading water, trying to flash each other signals with our eyes.

You can pin me!

No, you can pin me!

Here's my knee!

Here's my head!
I don't even do push-ups.
These hands are nature's pillows!

It was a stalemate. But in the second round I started with an advantage.

There are three starting positions in wrestling. There's

1. I hump you.
2. You hump me.
3. Who humps whom? (That's called "neutral.")

I was in the "I hump you" and the ref blew the whistle and somehow, and I do not know how to this very day, I found myself pinning this guy.

I couldn't believe it. My opponent couldn't believe it. My teammates really couldn't believe it. They jumped off the bench. They shouted, "Mike, squeeze!" Which, in wrestling, means "squeeze!"

So I was squeezing and squeezing. And I noticed there was all this blood on the mat. I thought, *Oh no, I killed this guy. I'm gonna be on the run for the rest of my life. They'll say, "Birbiglia the wrestling bandit. One pin, one kill! Couldn't do a single push-up but he murdered a guy with his bare hands."*

Then I realized that it was my own blood streaming out of my nose onto the mat based on no injury whatsoever. Just from the sheer nervousness of possibly winning anything at all.

The ref blew the whistle and shouted, "Blood on the mat!" which was redundant. A little blood boy ran out and he wiped it up with a rag, then jogged off and threw it into the blood castle.

My teammates plugged my nose. They said, "Mike, get out there and do what you just did." I had no idea what I had just done.

I walked back onto the mat and struck the "I hump you" position and the ref blew the whistle, and as quickly as I had pinned this guy, I myself was pinned.

That was the closest I would ever come to winning a wrestling match.

As embarrassing and pride swallowing as that sounds, I remember it to this very day, and I'm glad that I did it. I'm glad that after I lost again and again and again in increasingly embarrassing ways, I still showed up. I was building character.

I was pulling myself onto the ottoman.

I was trying.

*

When my daughter learns to use the toilet

...we sing to her poops to coax them into this world:

Come out come out come out little poop
And say hello to daughter and me
Come out come out come out little poop
And say hello to mommy and me

My daughter poops a treasure more valuable to Earth,
says Earth,
than any contribution of the high arts.

*

THE LEGS DON'T
REACH THE FLOOR

One night we're sitting on the couch and I say to Jen, "I feel like I'm trying so hard and it's not helping."

Jen says, "You try hard for me but it's not for Oona. You don't try hard for us."

I pull out my laptop and start surfing travel sites. This is something I know how to do. I'm a professional traveler. I'm sick of being the vice president of the family. I think, *I will plan a family vacation and be promoted to president.*

This will be our "babymoon," but this time everyone will show up.

I email all my co-workers: "I will be away for the next two weeks."

I plan a family vacation to the beach.

My fondest memories of childhood vacations took place on the beach. When my parents took us, it was one of my first experiences of pure joy. Going in the ocean. Experiencing that sensation where you can't see your feet, and at any moment a shark or a fish or a crab might swim by and you wouldn't even know. My mom always used to point out that the ocean was medicinal. She's a nurse. She'd say that if you had a cut from falling down on the pavement that you could go into the ocean for a few days and it might not be cured but it would be on its way to healing.

I book my family flights, a rental car, and a beachside hotel room in California. The travel websites are so desperate to sell you more stuff: *You wanna add a rental car? How 'bout some cig-arettes? What about an old-fashioned bicycle with that super-big wheel? How about a kickboxing lesson with my uncle Fred? How about you don't bring your family on this trip at all?*

I splurge on a fancy hotel on the beach in Santa Monica.

We fly across the country. We're carrying a stroller and sixteen suitcases and three baggies of bananas and Cheddar Bunnies and sippy cups. Oona is screaming and people are staring at us but now I'm flashing them looks like, *How dare you judge this baby who wants to see the world!*

We pick up our rental car in Long Beach, and the rental agency hadn't installed the car seat. They just plopped it in the back seat, which is like giving someone an Ikea nightstand for their birthday with a note that says, "You figure it out."

It's pouring.

I take out my phone and find a YouTube instructional video for putting in car seats. It's some camp-counselor-looking guy with a British accent, saying, "Three simple steps. You strap, latch, and cinch!"

I'm shouting at my phone as I hold the car seat parts: "You cinch WHAT?!" Oona's screaming.

The British camp counselor says, "Now that it's installed, you can shake the car by just shaking the car seat."

"But it's not installed! Slow down! We're not all British Car Seat Fucking Superheroes."

Jen says, "I can do this in five seconds." She pushes me aside, then straps, latches, and cinches. Uncle Googlemaps tells us it'll take twenty minutes to get to our hotel, but, since it's rained only several times in Los Angeles in the last century, the city is in chaos and it takes an hour and forty minutes.

We arrive at the hotel at ten o'clock at night. We're in a room with a queen bed and a pullout couch. With my sleepwalking, I have to sleep in a separate bed. But when I try to pull out the couch, it won't *pull out*. There are couches that hug you. But this is not that.

I'm using the wall as leverage to pull out the bed, and it finally pulls out but the legs won't reach the floor. I call the front desk.

I say, "Hey, could someone take a look at our pullout couch?"

The hotel engineer walks in a few minutes later and tinkers with it. He pretty much does the same few experiments that I had done but with more confidence. Then he says, "I can't fix that couch."

I say, "Do you know anyone who could?"

He says, "There's not much you can do. The metal on the legs is bent."

I say, "Right, I didn't do that. Do I look like the metal-bending type? I'm the pizza-bending type or the yoga-mat-bending type but not the metal-bending type."

Oona's asleep.

Jen says, "I don't think I'm going to be able to sleep on that couch."

I say, "That's fine, I'll sleep on it."

She says, "No, you can't, because of your sleepwalking."

I say, "What do you want me to do?! I can't leave my own body. I'm stuck with this. There's no cure for me."

I decide to appeal to the front desk. I bolt out of the room for the elevator. The people at the front desk can tell how angry I am from forty feet away. It must have seemed like my eyebrows were angled off my head like a cartoon.

I'm rushing through the lobby. The bellman crashes into me with that cart thing and it almost tips over. I say to the man at the front desk, "We have a pullout couch in our room that doesn't touch the floor in any way. There is nothing that makes it furniture. I was very clear that I needed two working beds!"

He types away at the computer for ten minutes to give the illusion of progress and then says, "We don't have any other rooms."

I am speechless. I don't know what to do. I return to our defective hotel room. Jen and Oona are cuddled up in the bed, asleep. I lie on the pullout. There's a bar pushing into my back as I try to sleep. This combined with Oona screaming starts infusing into my dreams. Every time I nod off, I start to have this dream that my daughter's scream is a fire alarm, and I fear, as I lie in bed half-asleep, that I'll try to throw her through the window.

I don't sleep.

The sun comes up, and it's that infuriating feeling when you haven't slept and the sun comes up and you think, *But I didn't do the thing!*

I get out of bed and Jen suggests that we walk down to the beach.

She opens the glass sliding door in the room and I hobble over to the doorway and step onto the beach. I haven't had coffee so I can barely open my eyes. Oona jogs onto the sand and says, "San.'" This is why we've come all this way. As we walk towards the water I step on something sharp. I look down and see a plastic lighter just sitting there on the sand.

I look a few feet to the right and there's a bottle cap.

I look around and there's a Starbucks cup and a used condom.

I realize there's garbage all over the beach from the storm the night before.

The shoreline is a zigzag line of seaweed and stones mixed with plastic bottles and candy wrappers and lighters and . . . then what really sets me off . . . is an empty can of tuna fish.

This idea that we're consuming so much that we're throwing the excess back into the place where the fish live. I think, *My God. There are actual tuna fish in the ocean trying to make it work and you're gonna throw an empty can of their dead brother into their own house?*

Oona reaches for this sharp, rusty can of tuna fish and I tackle her.

And I start crying.

I'm trying and failing and the earth is burping garbage. *Fuck.*

A few days later we board our return flight. I have not been deemed a hero. I have not been elected president of our home.

*

A toast to something beautiful flapping in the wind

To something beautiful flapping in the wind above the beach houses—A blue bird?—No, a blue bag.

To her breath—raindrops in the begonia bed. My eyesight is rainstorms.

Drop,

drop—

To 4am, her first ocean—
Everyone is sleeping except Oona and the ocean,
Oona and the ocean.

I try to explain in whale song I try to explain in rainstorm. Cloud and water droplet.

Drop,

drop—

Spending time with a baby is like spending time with something that has lived in an ocean her entire life and just sprouted legs for land—

I am like Copernicus using the planet of my body to umbrella the wind as she feeds—Ouch! I stick my fingers in her mouth and she's grown sharp little fish teeth—

Drop,

Everyone is sleeping
except Oona and the ocean,
Oona and the ocean and the little fish teeth.

Drop,

drop,

drop,

drop,

I tell time by counting teeth-marks around the crooked nipple.

IT IS WHAT IT IS

I wake up at 5:30 a.m. on a Saturday to drive to Potsdam, New York, for a gig at Clarkson University.

I make coffee and pour it into a mug that dons the phrase "it is what it is." This is part of an ensemble of mugs my mom had given to me and Jen at Christmas. Mine says "it is what it is" and Jen's says "follow your heart." If I followed my heart, it wouldn't lead me to Potsdam, New York, so I guzzle some watery coffee from "it is what it is."

Uncle Googlemaps insists that it's a six-and-a-half-hour drive, but Uncle Googlemaps has not visited the far reaches of New York State. He has only photographed it from afar. A drive to Albany is a quick jaunt on the New York State Thruway. The voyage to Potsdam *could take days*. It takes you from I-87 to Routes 28 to 30 to 56 and, at some point along the way, it takes you through the West Canada Lake Wilderness, which isn't even in Canada but might give you the sense that we are pretty far from home. Or anywhere.

Joe is concerned about me doing the whole drive myself, so he offers to join me. I insist that we stop for a meal two hours from the show and check into our hotel room, drive two more hours, do the show, and then drive two hours back to our hotel room afterwards.

Joe thinks this is a bad idea because—it is a bad idea.

But I insist. I have this distinct feeling of guilt whenever I'm away from Jen and Oona, so I always make plans for how to get home faster.

By the time we get to Clarkson I'm so exhausted that I can't even imagine walking onstage.

It's 8:50 p.m. The show is at 9:30.

I say to the students who had booked me, "Is there a dressing room?"

"We don't have that."

"Do you have a private room with a couch?"

"Pretty sure we don't have that."

"Is there a private room with a door handle?"

"Yes!"

They take me to an empty room and I turn off the lights and then lie down on an industrial-carpeted floor.

For the next forty minutes, the door opens every ninety seconds. A wide stream of light blares in. Then the door closes. These intermittent disturbances happen with such regularity that I start to get the sense that the word has gotten around campus: "If you open that door, you can see a comedian sleeping on a floor." It's possible that someone is even charging admission. That person may be my brother, Joe.

After forty minutes on the floor, I stand up and perform an hour of comedy that starts at 9:30, and then we set off around 11:00 p.m. After the show, I insist on driving. But on the drive home we hit torrential rains, and white-knuckle driving ensues. The rain crashes down so hard on the windshield that the sound is mesmerizing, and it starts to suggest ways I might want to drive my car into the "West Canada Lake Wilderness."

That's when I know I need to pull over.

Joe and I hop out of the car in the pouring rain to trade places. I instantly fall asleep in the passenger seat and Joe drives the rest of the way to the hotel.

At 1:00 a.m., after an eleven-hour travel day and a stand-up comedy show, Joe wakes me up and I groggily head to my room.

It's on the second floor, and I'm on the phone with Jen and she's worried. She can hear in my voice that I'm on the edge. There's a level of fatigue I sometimes hit where Jen can feel a sleepwalking incident coming on.

Jen coaches me on where to put the furniture in the room. She suggests that I push a dresser in front of the window and an armchair in front of that. I am Birbiglia-proofing the room. We do our best, but we both know it's not a good situation.

I take my medication. I slide into my sleeping bag and fall asleep.

I have a dream that I'm in that scene from *Indiana Jones and the Temple of Doom* where the walls are closing in and I sprint away as I hear a musical composition that sounds like the score to the end of my life. And these dreams, when I have them, feel as real as anything in my waking life.

I sprint away, but I'm wearing a sleeping bag so my legs are stuck and my face smacks against the floor like a flyswatter. My face is skinned and bleeding and I'm waking up realizing *I'm not in the Temple of Doom...I'm in upstate New York.*

I hobble back to bed, because...what am I gonna do? I can't go to the front desk and say, "I have a complaint about my dreams."

The next morning I wake up and the sheets are covered in blood.

I meet Joe at the breakfast buffet. We don't say much over eggs and toast, but finally Joe says, "I don't like the safety profile of that trip last night."

I say, "I don't like the safety profile of my life."

That morning I write in my journal: "I don't know if I'll live much longer."

There's something in the lack of control I'm feeling that is new. And scary. I'm barely sleeping. I'm having these sleepwalking incidents that feel like the one that nearly killed me, and the person I'm closest to in the world is dealing with a struggle of her own: raising our child.

When I get home I crash on our bed and Jen comes in.

I say, "I wrote in my journal that I think I might die soon. Like Mitch or Greg. I'm embarrassed to tell you that, but I thought you should know."

Jen says, "I'm sorry. I used to be able to protect you in these situations, but I'm spread too thin right now and I don't know what to do."

We hold on to each other in bed. The undercurrent of panic in my consciousness subsides for a few moments, but we both know that there's nothing either of us can do.

Oona won't sleep.

Jen can't sleep.

I'm sleepwalking.

We are all rooting for each other.

I'm thirty-five pounds overweight.

We all want to be together.

We can't always be together.

It is what it is.

VII.

ME AND MY WIFE ON A PLANE THAT'S CRASHING

My worst nightmare is being in a plane crash with my wife because somehow I feel like I would be blamed for the plane crash.

We'll find out we're going down and she'll look at me and say, "I told you we shouldn't have gone on this flight." And I'll say, "First of all you *didn't* say we shouldn't go on this flight. Second of all we're visiting your parents in Florida. I didn't want to do either of those things. I didn't wanna visit your parents in Florida and I didn't want to die in this plane crash."

She'll say, "Never mind, doesn't matter."

I'll say, "Okay, but it does matter because you literally just told me we shouldn't have gone on this flight, and that didn't happen."

She'll say, "You know I hate going on planes."

I'll say, "Right, but everybody hates going on planes. You can't own the idea of 'hating going on planes.'"

She'll say, "Whenever we fly I'm always telling you that we're gonna crash."

I'll say, "Again, that's the risk you always assume when you fly in a plane and everything in life really is a risk-and-reward situation and in this case the reward was going to be seeing your parents and the risk was that we could die and as it turns out, we're going to die. So I don't even think we should talk about it anymore. I think we should just spend the last ten minutes of our lives enjoying each other's company since we are deeply in love and I wish to spend the final minutes of my life with you in peace."

She'll say, "That's what I wanted to do."

I'll say, "Actually you didn't."

She'll say, "It doesn't matter. It literally doesn't matter. Oh, look—it seems like they might be able to land the plane."

I'll say, "Do you know if you can order an Uber to a field?"

She'll say, "I don't use Uber anymore because of the way they underpay their employees. There was that one story in the *Times* about that driver committing suicide."

I'll say, "Right, but if it's the only way to get out of the field, I think we should make an exception."

She'll say, "It's up to you. I don't care."

I'll say, "But you just said you care."

She'll say, "Well...I would just appreciate it if we could try Lyft first and if Lyft isn't available then we can do Uber."

In conclusion, my greatest fear is being on a crashing plane with my wife and knowing that I am right and being told that I am wrong and then dying.

VIII.

CAN I HAVE THIS HOUSE WHEN YOU DIE?

One Christmas, when I was twelve, I said to my parents while sitting by the fireplace, "Mom and Dad, can I have this house when you die?"

When you die.

I was more comfortable with my parents' deaths than I was with parting with our cozy, medium-sized home, built by Bob Cole in 1978, the year of my birth.

I loved that house. I wanted to live there forever. That said, there was a tree outside our window that my parents must have planted when I was born. It was a small, flowering tree. My window was about twenty feet above the ground and the tree was about thirteen feet high. And I always had this fantasy that someday the tree would grow tall enough that I could climb out the window and leave our house. I don't even know where I was planning to go. But the tree never grew high enough. And eventually we moved. And I recently visited Shrewsbury and I went for a walk to my childhood home. And there's the tree. And it's still not tall enough for someone to climb out the window. I think the moral of the story is: Don't wait for that fucking tree to grow. Because it's not going to.

It's Christmas 2015. Jen and Oona and I are visiting my parents at their current home in Cape Cod. I'm walking with my dad around the neighborhood. There's become increasingly less to talk about with my dad as we've gotten older.

My dad, or "Vince," as my family prefers to call him, was born and raised in Bushwick, Brooklyn, and caught a break when he scored well on an entrance exam for a Catholic high school in Manhattan called Xavier. From there he went to Holy Cross College and then University at Buffalo for medical school.

Holy Cross College forms the backdrop of many positive memories from my childhood. My dad used to take me and my best friend Michael Kavanagh to football games there every weekend in the fall when I was a kid. We would start the day eating lunch in the school cafeteria at the top of the hill, and we would slide down a series of grassy slopes until we reached the stadium. Along the way we'd accrue grass stains and knee scrapes and pull off imaginary game-winning catches in football plays with our mini purple Holy Cross football that my dad had bought us in the school bookstore. When we got to the stadium we would watch part of the game and then Michael Kavanagh and I would play pickup football in the grassy fenced-off area behind one of the end zones. Every half hour we'd take a break and fill up on hot dogs and popcorn and crazy crappy food that kept us powered up for another half hour.

My dad was always happy there. He was so proud that he had gone to Holy Cross. And I think he was equally proud when I graduated from a Catholic college as well. That feels like a long time ago, partly because it is and partly because there's a rift these days between my dad and me.

Vince is extremely smart but hasn't caught up to the fact that email forwards about American foreign policy from an account called TOMSGONEGOLFIN@AOL.COM aren't as legitimate as in-depth reporting by a war correspondent in the Democratic Republic of the Congo.

I bring up this particular example because my best friend from childhood, Michael Kavanagh, became a war correspondent in the Congo. And it's scary. And it keeps me up at night. So it rubs me the wrong way on this Christmas walk with my dad when, inevitably, we stumble into a discussion of current events and my dad says, "The media is the problem."

I say, "Dad, your son is in the media."

He says, "You're not really in the media."

I say, "I work in media. Secondly, Michael Kavanagh risks his life every day as a journalist so people can better understand the complexity of that part of the world."

That might sound less exciting than my dad's TV show of choice, *Mad Money*, but I'd venture to say that it's more noble than shouting into a TV camera about the stock market for an hour a day.

My dad isn't alone in writing off journalists. This is a current trend.

Email forwards can be a more pleasant resource.

Vince used to send them to us, too, but then one of them crossed the line for my brother, Joe.

In September of 2008, TOMSGONEGOLFIN@AOL.COM forwarded my dad a viral email that had bullet points with conspiracy theories about Barack Obama. One of them was:

HIS MOTHER IS KANSAN, ATHEIST, AND WHITE. SO—
WHERE ARE ALL THOSE PICTURES OF HIS NICE WHITE
MOTHER AND HIS NICE WHITE GRANDPARENTS—THE
ONES WHO RAISED HIM ALL THOSE EARLY YEARS?

Another one was:

SOMEHOW, SUDDENLY—HE WENT TO THE BEST HIGH
DOLLAR PREP SCHOOLS IN AMERICA, AND LATER HE
GOT INTO A TOP IVY LEAGUE COLLEGE AND LATER, INTO
HARVARD LAW SCHOOL—HOW? WHO SPONSORED HIM?
WHO PAID FOR ALL THAT SCHOOLING?

This email didn't go over well with anyone in my family. But it particularly crossed a line for Joe. He was angered at Vince, who at that time may not have understood that forwarding a chain email includes an implicit endorsement. My dad spent sixty years in a world without email, so the idea that he would understand all of its nuances was a bit of an unfair expectation. But it was something Joe was willing to teach him, and he did that by replying

directly to TOMSGONEGOLFIN@AOL.COM, cc'ing everyone on the email chain.

Joe addressed all thirteen bullet points. He started with:

> Tom,
>
> Let's talk about your email a bit:
>
> First off, there is a button called "caps lock," it should be to
> the left of the "a" key, you're going to want to press that, so
> you're not yelling all the time. I took the liberty of numbering
> your claims for easy reference:

Then Joe took on each claim one by one and refuted them
with facts. My favorite moment in Joe's email was when he
explained how Barack Obama might be funded.

> Barack Obama has written 2 books, which have sold millions
> of copies. I'm not sure millions of people want to purchase your
> CAPITALIZED EMAIL RANTS.

This email from Joe was not well received. It created tension
in my family for months if not years. But it's an example of why
our family simply can't discuss current events. We don't believe
in the same truth. Vince believes email forwards more than he
believes journalism.

It's seven years later and I'm walking with my dad.

I accidentally stumble into a conversation about journalism,
and my dad quotes something from one of these pass-along
emails he recently received. He spouts off one of these theories
that I know not to be true and so I cite a fact that I know about
that specific theory.

And he says, "I didn't know that."

I say, "Right, because they don't fact-check email forwards."

My dad walks in silence for a few minutes, stewing. Then he says, "You've really gone another way."

That was the end of the conversation. The next day Jen and Oona and I headed home.

Since then Vince and I have had positive conversations where we don't bring up current events. But we both know that these differences between us lie beneath the surface and that one false move from either of us could turn into a very tense conversation. And I know that my dad is in the latter half of his life. He's had more than one heart attack and this year battled a painful bout of pancreatitis. So we both know that it's possible that a tense political conversation could end up being our last. And I don't want that to happen.

I think that's why I can't get that childhood line out of my head: *Can I have this house when you die?*

It seemed so logical at the time, but now it makes me sad. I don't connect with that statement anymore. We've long since moved from that house. I have no personal attachment to the house my parents live in now, and I certainly don't want them to die.

I'm driving home with Jen and Oona and thinking about how Oona will someday be my age and I will hopefully be my father's age and I may not grasp something Oona's telling me because I simply can't.

If and when that happens, I hope she'll be able to separate that difference in opinion from love. But there's no way to be certain.

My dad will die. Everyone does. And I hope it's not on a day when we disagree about current events. But it might be. And I don't know what to do about it. My dad's not going to change. But I won't wait for that tree to grow. I won't wait for my parents to die.

So I'm writing it here:

Dad, I love you.

No, wait. I'll say it in all caps:

I LOVE YOU. I APPRECIATE EVERYTHING YOU'VE DONE FOR ME. AND I'LL ALWAYS REMEMBER OUR DAYS AT HOLY CROSS COLLEGE IN THE FALL.

IX.

SO WE DON'T CRY

One night in February of 2016 I'm sitting on the couch with Jen watching the movie *Spotlight*.

I'm crying. A lot. That kind of crying where if you were in a car in the rain you'd have to pull over. I'm crying so hard that I actually have to pause the movie—for fifteen minutes.

The moment in the film that breaks me is when a man, sitting in a diner, reveals to a reporter that he was molested by a priest when he was a child. There's something about this scene that is so vivid and real and painful that despite the countless articles and documentaries I've seen on this subject, this is the scene that breaks me. Maybe it has something to do with the fact that I now have a daughter. I don't know.

I'm crying so hard that Jen asks me if I was abused as a child. I wasn't. I was an altar boy. I even have a joke about it: "I was an altar boy as a kid and the answer is...No. I wasn't. I think it's because they knew I was a talker."

This joke usually gets a big laugh, but it's also the joke that has provoked my most hecklers over the years. One night in Boston, I told this joke and a man in the audience shouted, "Come on!"

To which I replied, "What do you mean come on?"

He said, "Haven't we heard that enough?"

I'm not sure we have.

I think what I respect most about *Spotlight* is that it doesn't shy away from the topic at all. It deliberately shines a light on events without apology or fear. I think comedy can do this as well. I think sometimes comedians are able to tell the truth about things other people won't talk about.

There's a George Bernard Shaw quote where he says, "When you want to tell people the truth, make them laugh. Otherwise they'll kill you."

But "make them laugh" isn't universally agreed upon. Some people don't want the comedian to rain on their lighthearted comedy parade. And other people feel that jokes about sensitive topics normalize the behavior.

It's a complex problem, I get it. The normalizing argument is compelling.

A few years ago, when driving in Los Angeles, I was T-boned by a drunk driver on the driver's side and it nearly killed me. The drunk driver's car struck an inch from my head. It was traumatic. A year later, a comedian opened for me and, not knowing this, told a joke about drunk driving. Something to the effect of, "Don't drive drunk . . . unless you're having a really good time."

This joke got me thinking: *Does his joke about drunk driving normalize drunk driving?*

I don't know the answer. Maybe it does. I can't be certain. But it's also possible that it starts a conversation between a couple in the audience who is sharing a car home about who should drive. I'm afraid of normalizing abuse, but I'm also afraid of normalizing silence. I'd guess there aren't a lot of jokes in cults about the cult leader sleeping with all the women and their daughters. But I'm guessing the silence that surrounds the abuse might perpetuate it.

In 2015, a film came out called *Call Me Lucky*. It's a documentary directed by Bobcat Goldthwait that follows the life of the late great comedian Barry Crimmins, who was sexually abused and raped as a child. He talks about it candidly in the film and onstage as a comedian.

In defense of his own sensitive material, Crimmins says, "If these kids had to live it, you could at least say the words out loud."

His final statement in the documentary is: "We have to take care of innocents in this world and we have to be brave enough to tell the truth about innocents in this world. So tell the truth. Tell everyone the truth. Tell anyone the truth. Because your lives depend on it. My life depends on it. And people who really can't be heard really depend on it."

I think the goal of jokes is to make us laugh and hopefully open up the conversation to topics we don't really want to discuss. Can a joke be a spotlight in the darkness? Can a joke make room for a discussion of that darkness?

I'm sitting with Jen on the couch as we turn the movie back on. Oona is asleep in the other room. I'm thinking about the heckler in Boston. I can't get his words out of my head.

"Haven't we heard that enough?"

I'm not sure we have.

X.

525,600 PHOTOS

A day before Oona's first birthday, Jen assembles a photo slide-show of our daughter's first year, a last-ditch effort for us to prove to Oona's relatives that we are decent parents.

As Jen and I lie in bed scrubbing through photos on her phone she pauses to make an observation: "I took all the photos."

I say, "No, you didn't."

I pull out my laptop. Over the next sixteen hours, I look through my iPhoto and find 4,326 photos and 345 videos of Oona totaling seven and a half hours. The way I sort through the photos is with a facial-recognition software called Faces that comes standard with every Apple computer. It's terrifying. I identify my daughter's face as "Oona" in one photo and then it presents me with 3,000 other possible photos of Oona. My computer turns into a creepy magi-cian. *"Is this your child? Is this your child? I want you to pick a child, and remember that child, and I'm going to put that child back in with the photos…Is this your child?"*

The whole thing feels like the inciting incident in a sci-fi thriller about duplicating Oonas. I fear that at some point iPhoto will say, "We've gathered enough data, Michael. Would you like to 3-D print another Oona?" I saw the eighties film *Weird Science*, and they basically printed a lady, and my computer is ten thousand times more powerful than the computer those guys had.

I sit down on the green/gray couch and watch hours of these videos.

June 25, 2015—Oona is two months old, her arms and legs

move like an animatronic doll. She sneezes, not knowing what a sneeze is, momentarily concerned that her head has exploded.

July 7, 2015—Jen is in front of our house securing Oona into a stroller. The stroller, which was a gift from Jen's brother Jordan, will be stolen in two months. We won't mention that to Jordan. His copy of this book is redacted.

August 30, 2015—Me and Oona on this very couch. She is leaning on my knees and grasping my finger. A mess of toys and baby junk litters the living room floor in the background. I sing in an operatic voice: ♪♫ *"It's a knee party/ A knee party/ for my Oona/ A knee party/ A knee party/ for my Oona!!"* ♪♫

Her eyes are widening. I'm a new musician and she's a new baby. She's a better baby than I am a musician.

January 5, 2016—Oona is nine months old. Jen is off camera saying, "Oona, what does Dad do?" Oona smiles. Jen says, "Does he gesticulate? Can you gesticulate like Dad?" Oona does a spot-on physical impression of me flapping my arms around. She's the only toddler who knows the word "gesticulate."

March 20, 2016—I play guitar in Oona's bedroom and she dances. The floor of the room is covered in playmats and pillows to soften her falls. I'm making up the words as I go:

♪♫ *"She loves her mom . . . and she loves her dad . . . and she loves her hat . . . and she loves her cat . . . But she hates to sleep . . . And we don't know why . . . She hates to sleep . . . Because she hates goodbyes."* ♪♫

I notice something in these videos for the first time. My songs have come a long way from "Hiccuptown." I notice something else: Not only do I witness my daughter evolve from the size of a crawling grapefruit to the size of a walking watermelon like a stop-motion animation. But I also see Jen's reaction to Oona and I see mine. Jen's reaction is that of a person watching a part of her own body break free and then, eventually, learn how to drink from a cup. My reaction is that of someone who is happy for my wife, but also afraid. I'm afraid that our marriage may never be the same.

I'm proud of my cinematic accomplishment. I was right. I took thousands of photos and I have the evidence to prove it. I present this evidence to Jen. She says, "It's nice that you assembled these photos but the truth is—I took most of these. You can tell because a majority of them are me capturing you and Oona. The ones of just Oona and me are close-ups. They're selfies."

Jen guides me through her photos: "I have great footage of you singing to Oona. Her biting your nose and the both of you giggling. Her playing your belly like a drum. But the candid footage of Oona and I connecting in this way doesn't exist."

I say, "What about all the photos I sent you?"

Jen says, "Seventy percent of your photos are shots that I took and sent to you."

"But…"

I struggle to respond.

I say, "What about the one I just showed you? The video of you putting Oona in the stroller, you couldn't have shot that!"

Jen pivots to the death blow. It's the first time I can see that Jen feels hurt that I haven't documented her growth with Oona.

She says, "I made sure to capture the magic moments between the two of you. I don't feel like you captured that for us. I shot principal photography of Oona's first year. And you shot B roll."

The Cup

It's not that I'm jealous of water when she drinks it—

It's just the way the cup covers most of her face as she brings it to her lips—The way my boob would cover most of her face before she could speak and she'd sing along with my singing with the wideness of her blueberry eyes—It's the same now—She will have a conversation with only her eyes, or a nod of the head, her face swallowed up mostly by a cup as she drinks—

It's not the water that brings these pangs of envy as much as the flash of an expression from behind the cup.

✱

XI.

NATURAL CAUSES

SUGAR FRIES

We have a party for Oona's first birthday.

We were never going to have a party. We barely celebrate our own birthdays. Oona won't remember it happened. We won't get the stains off the couch. No one wins. But then it happened. We had a children's birthday party. It cost about a half million dollars and I think someone stole my umbrella, but it's over and that's the best thing about children's birthday parties: They end.

As the guests are leaving, one of the moms says to Jen, "You know, the first birthday isn't for the kid, it's for the mom."

Jen starts crying.

Perhaps they are the tears of all the birthdays of her own she never celebrated. Perhaps they are tears of joy that we've made it through the first year, or perhaps they're tears of pure exhaustion from the three and a half hours of sleep she patched together the night before. Whoever the party is for, it's a happy birthday.

Oona is one year old.

I am almost forty.

Some people pull off forty pretty well. I don't feel like I'm gonna be one of those people. I'm gonna be a hard forty. I'm gonna be a forty where people say, "Are you fifty?" I'll say, "No, but thanks for adding a decade of decay and no wisdom to my life!" Forty is big. And scary. It's exactly halfway through your life. Not technically. Not everyone dies at eighty, but no one's ever like, "Eighty through one hundred. Those are the years!" They say things like, "I was eighty-three and I reached for a grape and I never walked again."

The expression for forty is "over the hill." I never understood that idea until I climbed up the hill and looked around. I thought, *Oh! There's natural causes! They're not close, but they're coming!*

I walk into the bathroom to shower off the birthday germs and I step on my scale: a new all-time high. I look at my calendar and see that I've gained twenty-two pounds in the last two years. *Jesus. How did this happen?*

I've taken sympathetic eating to the extreme. My sympathy has expanded my belt size and thickened my neck.

The next day I visit my doctor and he takes blood.

Two days later I'm working in Columbus, Ohio. My doctor calls me and says, "I got your results. You have type 2 diabetes. I'd like to put you on medication."

I say, "I really don't want to take medication since I already take the Klonopin for sleep. I'd prefer to try to change my eating habits."

He says, "Well, I don't know... It would have to be drastic. You'd have to cut out red meat, sugar, fries..."

That's when I start thinking about "sugar fries," which isn't a thing—but it should be. It's a match made in heaven. Sugar. Fries. Plus, it has an obvious theme song: ♪ *Sugar fries, sugar fries, sugar fries, sugar fries in my eyes!* ♪

I get off the phone with my doctor and lie in my hotel bed, ruminating on my own mortality. I had cancer when I was nineteen. Diagnosed with a sleepwalking disorder at twenty-five. But here I am at age thirty-seven with what somehow feels like the beginning of the end.

I'm addicted to food. I'm addicted to work and stress. None of this helps.

Food, with the right combination of salt and sugar, causes my body to feel like it is pressing a button. Once I do it I feel better. It's usually after a series of events that seem out of my control. Let's say I spend the day sprinting to make a flight in traffic and then sprinting to the gate to catch the flight and then sprinting to the rental car agency and there aren't enough cars and then I have to scramble to find public transportation and then eventually I get to the gig and everyone in the audience hates me.

That is out of my control.

Do you know what's in my control? Sugar fries.

I'm lying in this hotel bed in Ohio and I turn on the TV. I watch all these ads for mysterious medications that apparently we should ask our doctors about. The ads feature a series of elderly actors who are apparently *thrilled* to ask. *Am I going to be one of those people soon? Am I going to be popping unknown pills and be thrilled about it?*

I hit the minibar. I've spent a lot of time rooting through hotel minibars and I've never purchased the little alcohol bottles but I'm triple digits on glass jars of peanut M&M's.

If you suck on a peanut M&M long enough, it's just a peanut. If you suck on that peanut long enough, you can taste pure shame. But that feeling of shame eventually turns to pride. You think, *This is actually pretty healthy. I've been meaning to eat more nuts.* Then you pop a couple hundred of those and you get a sugar high. You think, *I should run a marathon!*

And then you don't.

And then you get type 2 diabetes—which is an unfortunate outcome.

I'm sucking on a peanut M&M, flipping channels. I see a commercial for heartburn medication and all I can think is *That pizza looks so good. I gotta get some of that heartburn-medication-brand pizza. I don't know if that's what they're getting at, but I am in.*

I lower the volume on the TV and FaceTime with Jen and Oona before Oona goes to bed. FaceTiming is an activity that, with a one-year-old child, you might as well not bother trying. You're just this loud, two-dimensional image of a dad. You're a cartoon but less colorful, shiny, and fun. I start to tell Jen about my dramatic call with my doctor, but, before I can get into it, Oona accidentally presses "end."

That seems about right. We'll be witnessing the end sooner than expected if Dada doesn't get his shit together.

I shut off my phone as I suck on the inside of a peanut M&M.
I think, *Something's gotta change.*

I order a pizza. I'll need some energy to implement this new
plan.

*

wean

a little
less and
a little less and a little

less and then
no more.

but tonight, a little more.

a little
less and
a little less and a little

less and then
no more.

but tonight, a little, a little more.

*

ORGANIC TOXIC WASTE

Part of my new health regimen is that every Sunday I walk three thousand steps to Whole Foods.

The activity serves multiple purposes. At one year old Oona eats solid foods and at age thirty-seven I start to eat vegetables. Plus, I'm doing something tangible for the family while Jen is putting Oona to bed. I also get some steps in since the doctor suggested I try to walk fifteen thousand steps per day.

Every time I make this trip it's not lost on me that I'm walking across the Gowanus Canal, which has been called by some "the most polluted waterway in the world." I skip past this toxic canal to pick up some *organic vegetables*.

That part isn't lost on me either.

But Jen is intent on *organic vegetables*.

She sends me articles about how the government is lifting regulations on chemicals that are causing health problems in children.

One night, a few weeks before, the organic store was closed, and Jen asked me to pick up some fruits and vegetables so I went to the *nonorganic* but *also very expensive* grocery store and returned home with nonorganic fruit. I don't remember if it was raining that night but it was certainly raining in my heart when Jen said, "Didn't you read the article I sent you?"

But I also get it. We might as well strive for a food product that isn't doused with chemicals. Especially since we have a child. She's got a long life ahead of her. I'll eat the poison apples, but she might prefer some nutrients.

That said, I'm skeptical of the whole "natural food" industry. I really don't believe things whose proof of their naturalness is a sticker. I feel like a lot of people could just buy a sticker and place it on any old banana. What's further confusing is that the organic fruit generally looks worse than the other fruit. But apparently that's part of the brand: "We didn't paint the bananas yellow; that's why they're brown."

I grab a cart and walk the aisles of the Whole Foods. I look at my list and start to choose some items: organic avocados, organic lettuce, organic bananas, organic apples—all the while sending photos to Jen to ask if it's the right type of organic food item. When the history books are written, there will be millions of photos of husbands and wives posing with various types of cereal and vegetables to find out whether their spouses think this purchase is a good idea. By the time those history books are written I think we may also be laughing heartily at the idea of "organic vegetables" for reasons we don't yet understand. Nevertheless, I press on.

I grab some organic milk, which I assume is from organic cows, which means the cows are alive. I've always felt it is important to get your milk from cows that are alive. I start to think that maybe milk will be my way into the family. Jen's whole thing is breast milk but maybe my angle is purchased milk. I think, *Right now she's reliant on breast milk but that could change. I could take Oona to the store. Show her around the milk section. I'd say, "What can I get ya? Chocolate milk? Strawberry milk? Five gallons of milk? Dada's going to hook you up! We could even take photos for Mama and text them to her. It could be our little inside joke: me and Oona. Dada's willing to forget that you ignored him for your entire life so far. Did I mention that purchased milk is gonna taste better than Mama's milk? Mama's milk is all squirts and dribbly. This is gonna be a steady stream of the good stuff. Organic milk from cows who are alive!"*

I make my way to the coffee shop that is inside the Whole Foods. For some reason I'm already exhausted and need to fill up on some liquid false energy for the rest of my shopping spree. As I glide through the aisles with my cart, it strikes me that 80 percent of what I'm seeing will end up in a landfill. A vast majority of what I'm looking at is packaging: brightly colored blends of plastic, cardboard, and metal that in one way or another will end up in the Gowanus Canal. Grocery-themed confetti. Good thing I brought my own reusable bags, my empty gesture in this imploding planet that says "I'm doing my best!"

I swing by the cheese samples station. This is perhaps my favorite activity at the grocery store because you're eating cheese but somehow not paying for it or even feeling guilt for eating it. You think, *This is the exact amount of cheese I wanted and I didn't even have to purchase it.*

Over the years I've become an "every-aisle" shopper as opposed to a "specific-aisle" shopper. Specific-aisle shoppers are myopic. They're like, *Paper towels and cereal, now get out of my way!* Every-aisle shoppers are like, *Isn't life really just a trip to the grocery store?* I used to be a specific-aisle shopper and then I had a few incidents where I'm home and it's eleven o'clock at night and I think, *Oh no. Graham crackers.* An every-aisle shopper is basically mowing the lawn that is the grocery store while sipping coffee and popping cheese samples. It's not a bad life.

I gulp down my coffee as I head to the checkout counter.

The woman at the register scans my Organic Girl organic butter lettuce. She looks me in the eye and says, "What does 'organic' even mean?"

I panic.

I sputter and stutter and say something to the effect of "My wife sent me this article about chemicals and..."

I look up and see that she's not really listening.

She says, "What?"

I say, "That's what my wife wants."

The look of judgment from this Whole Foods cashier is as mean as any bully I've ever encountered. And she sells organic food for a living. I think, *She was supposed to convince me to buy fraudulent overpriced vegetables, not the other way around.*

The cashier asks if I have the Whole Foods app on my phone and I pull out the app and I run it under the machine. I have earned a savings of $3.10 plus thirty cents for bringing my own bags. I've bought $120 worth of possibly organic fruits and vegetables, but I've saved enough money for a slice of nonorganic pizza.

I exit the store and walk across the toxic brown Gowanus Canal with my reusable brown bags filled with organic brown vegetables. I'm feeding my family and saving the planet. One step at a time.

YMCA

When Oona is a year old, we take her to Cape Cod to visit my parents. I bring her to the neighborhood swimming pool.

Seeing Oona in a pool is an activity that defies my own cynicism about children. It's enough to make the Grinch celebrate Christmas seven days a week. Oona loves the water. She loves that it splashes. She loves that she floats. She loves that Dada does silly things like hop onto the edge of the pool like a seal.

Jen is watching us from a lounge chair beside the pool and laughing.

"Clo, you can take an hour to yourself while we swim. I got this."

Jen says, "I can't. You don't know how to swim."

I say, "Yes, I do."

But I don't.

It doesn't occur to me until Jen says it that I actually have no technique whatsoever. I've been winging this swimming thing for years. But now my inadequate swimming has stakes. I can't be a liability in the water. I have to be a reliability. A buoy. A float. At the very least I need to be better at swimming than my one-year-old daughter.

Later that day we're driving back to New York and I'm stewing over the idea that I'm a bad swimmer and I decide I'm going to learn how to swim. The next day I walk into the YMCA for my first swim lesson in thirty years.

I have been actively avoiding the YMCA for decades.

When I was four years old, my mom took me into the women's locker room of the YMCA. I had never seen a vagina and then all of a sudden I saw one hundred. A year later she sent me into the men's locker room. The only thing more shocking than one hundred vaginas is one hundred penises at eye level. They were grown-up penises, which is a key detail because that aspect was particularly demoralizing. I thought, *Mine does not look like that. This is gonna be a long life.* So I looked around for child penises (please don't quote that out of context). I thought, *Phew. Everything's going to be okay.*

I never wanted to return to the YMCA. I can't identify the key turnoff. I don't know if it was the half-blown-up basketballs or the snack machine room with a coffee maker that also makes soup or the rowing machines that were also a fan that seemed to be powering the entire building.

Whatever it was, I didn't want to go back. But at this point I have no choice. I need to get better than my daughter at swimming.

As I approach my neighborhood YMCA in Brooklyn, I don't need directions. You can smell that chlorine stench for miles. They are not shy with their use of chlorine at the YMCA. It makes you think, *What the hell kind of heinous crime are they covering up? Are there Mafia hits in the middle of the night where the mobsters say, "What do we do with the corpse? Should we dig a ditch or do we bring the body down to the YMCA? I've got a family membership. We use a guest pass for the corpse. We drop the body in the pool and it'll disintegrate within six hours."*

I walk into the YMCA and meet with the swimming director Vanessa for a lesson.

She asks me where my swim cap is.

I say, "I don't have one. Sorry."

She says, "You have to wear a swim cap unless you're completely bald."

I think, *I don't like how she leaned on the word "completely." I am not even remotely bald. I have four distinct patches of hair that form the Voltron of hair atop my head.*

She says, "You can borrow my extra."

I put on Vanessa's extra swim cap, and now my head looks like a condom. Vanessa asks me to hop into the instructional lane and show her my "stuff." Full disclosure, I have no stuff. I hop in and flail around until I feel like I might die, and then I stand up.

The pool is Olympic sized and divided into lanes, but Vanessa has me in the walking lane. This is a pride-swallowing detail. And, to make matters worse, it's packed. There are three or four hundred water walkers. Only in New York City is there traffic in the pool. As I show Vanessa my flailing version of the crawl, these elderly walkers blow past me. I think one of them tried to dunk my head.

I say, "Vanessa, is it always this crowded?"

She says, "No, it's spring. Everyone is getting ready for the summer."

I say, "Oh. I get it." I point to my pumpkin-shaped frame and say, "They want a body *like this*!"

It's a joke.

Not stage-worthy material, but it's that sort of conversational repartee I use to forge a personal bond between myself and my swim instructor.

She doesn't hear it.

She says, "WHAT?"

I think, *I gotta get the hell out of this conversation.*

I say, "Doesn't matter."

She says, "Mike, I can't hear you. You have to shout!"

I say, *"VANESSA! THEY WANT A BODY LIKE THIS!"*

At this point my joke has lost all nuance and softness of cadence or any quality that could have helped make it humorous at all. A joke without comedic timing is a statement of pure insanity. All forty members of the pool look over at the pumpkin-shaped body attached to this confident voice. They stare at me as if to say, *Has this man seen his own body? There are so many mirrors at the YMCA.*

To be clear, I don't have a "swimmer's body." I have what I call a "drowner's body," where it seems like I'm drowning at all times even when I'm not near water. Even when I'm shirtless and dry, people are concerned.

At the end of my first lesson, I dry off with fifteen or twenty of those YMCA dish towels. I even stick two under my feet because Vanessa explains to me that "there's fungus in the puddles that can shoot straight into your veins through your feet."

I think, *This place is a death trap. I'm trying to get a little cardio in and now I'm mainlining fungus. It sounds like the only place they don't dump chlorine is in those puddles.*

So I'm at the YMCA wearing Vanessa's swim cap in the walkers' lane getting fungus shot into my veins while chlorine is surging up my nostrils. Then afterwards I'm so ravenous from swimming that I hit the snack machines and I'm eating Andy Capp's pub fries, which I'm pretty sure they haven't manufactured in the last twenty-five years.

I hop into the shower at the YMCA to get the heaps of chlorine and fungus off me and, embarrassingly, I keep on my bathing suit. There's something about those communal showers with no partitions that makes you feel like, *I'm as close to that other guy as if we were waiting in line at Chipotle except we're completely naked.*

Fifteen dish towels later I walk away from the YMCA, the smell of chlorine now emanating from my own body. At this point people in the street are walking towards me, thinking, *Is he the YMCA?* It's only my first swimming lesson, but it's an acceptance that I have turned the corner into middle age. I will not give up. Someday I will swim as well as my one-year-old, and that someday Jen will let me swim with Oona unsupervised.

From the YMCA we are born and into the YMCA we shall return.

*

Body, I never knew I could love you.

I never loved my body until she was inside it. I never loved my breasts until they made milk for her.

I never understood why people took naked pictures of themselves until she was inside me—The taut and expanding skin over the relentless womb. The anti-gravitational breasts—They are the only naked photos of myself you will find on my computer. Release them I don't care—release them for science.

I'll say it just once and only to myself—I do not want to give up the power to feed my child with my body—

I don't want to give up the power to be able to feed my child without a bowl or grain or utensil or dollar or bottle or government (this government) or job or faucet or jar—and on airplanes!—We are a smooth operating machine during takeoffs and landings—passengers come up to me and say your baby could solve world peace—she is the face of the ceasefire.

It scares me to depend completely on the world around us to feed my child. What if we get lost and I forget to pack snacks?—what if the economy dives and we have no money for food?—or a natural disaster?—or the dictator comes to power or some kind of attack?—or?—how will I feed her?

And what about these bouncy tits that knock together when I sex—I don't want to give them up.

*

SLICE OF LIFE

One day I take Oona to Sal's Pizzeria on our corner.

I order two slices and we sit at a table and eat.

She's thrilled.

I say, "Oona, do you like the pizza?"

She says, "Pi pi!" which I'm pretty sure means "pizza" and also "yes."

When we finish our slices she says, "Pi pi!"

She wants more pizza and also "yes."

I'm not quite sure what to do. Her mom said one slice but she didn't say anything about two slices. *How much pizza can a one-year-old eat?*

The battle cry grows stronger.

"Pi pi!!"

I can see this look in her eye that I recognize. She wants more pizza and she wants it *now*.

*

The Now-Clock

The now-clock is the clock of a toddler in which every number is replaced by the word "now" and the hands of the now are always pointed directly at the now or between two nows.

*

I have a pizza problem—which is to say that when I see a pizza I get excited. I perk up and think, *Oh! I'd like to have that inside of me!* I don't know if it's the circularity or the softness or the warmth, but it's almost sexual. I wouldn't have sex with pizza, but if I ate a pizza in private I wouldn't mention it to my wife.

I'm even excited by the word "pizza" because it *looks* like a pizza. Which is, of course, a literary device called "onomatopizza." Two *Z*s and an *A*. It's five slices in one word. I like pizza so much that I get excited when I see the word "plaza."

Jen has never called me out on looking at other women as we walk down the street, but she has called me out on looking at other pizza while I'm eating pizza.

It's a problem.

Because not only is it chock-full of sugar and salt and cheese and fat and bread, but I can only view a pizza as a single serving, when in fact, more often than not, it's designed for three or four people. That division somehow doesn't compute for me.

My brain thinks, *One pizza for one person. Pi pi!*

There is no logical way to partition a pizza. A typical configuration is three people sharing an eight-slice pie, which doesn't divide evenly. This is the subject of a documentary I'm working on called *Three People, Eight Slices.*

The three-person/eight-slice paradox is something pizza scholars have puzzled over for decades. You have three people and the first move is that everyone eats two slices and then awaits further instructions.

Hopefully there's a hero in the group who steps forward and says, "I'm not having any more." The proper etiquette is to genuflect in the direction of this deity. But if no one gives up their third slice, the only way to proceed is to cut the remaining two slices into thirds, giving each person two-thirds of one slice. You may need a fourth person to do the cutting if you want a fair cut. The pizza slicer is like a card dealer at a casino. Watch the hands.

Also, don't be fooled by what I call the "pizza racer," the guy who thinks that whoever *races* through his two slices first *wins* the third slice. And beware of the "salad negotiator"—this is someone who says something like, "Well, *you* had more salad," to which you must respond, "I will kill you with this salad fork."

Pizza for me is a sport. A sport for people who aren't good at sports.

My problem is enabled by my proximity to pizza. I live in Brooklyn, where there's a pizzeria on every corner. There's so much great pizza that even bad pizza tries to get in on the action. There's a Domino's Pizza right by my subway stop. Sometimes I fantasize about posting up in front of the Domino's all day and explaining other options to potential customers who could be paying the same amount for much better pizza.

And this is not meant to be judgmental. I don't believe there is such a thing as winners and losers in life. But I think if you live in Brooklyn and order pizza from Domino's you are a loser. I don't believe in heaven or hell, but I believe if you order a Brooklyn Domino's pizza you are going to hell. This is based in scripture. In the Old Testament, there is this passage where the serpent appears to Eve in the Garden of Eden. The serpent offers Eve a bite of his Domino's pizza. Eve says, "No thanks. God told me it's the worst pizza created in the last six days." The serpent says, "Look—it's 3:00 a.m. Nothing else is open." Eve takes a bite and that's why we're here. It was the original sin.

Beyond the perfection of the food item itself, pizza is a Band-Aid for so many problems:

I forgot to make dinner! Order a pizza.

I'm lonely. Order a pizza.

I have no utensils. Order a pizza.

Pizza is a food that I've called on in a jam my whole life. When I've been told by an audience that nothing I've presented to them is funny or entertaining, pizza has told me, *I liked it. And I like you.*

Pizza is not just a perfect blend of ingredients but of nostalgia, which can be the richest flavor of all. As a kid I spent countless afternoons with Michael Kavanagh and Matt Beaton playing scrappy backyard football and then eating way too much pizza at one of three Shrewsbury pizzerias within a half-mile radius.

Pizza and movies.

Pizza and friends.

Pizza and Jen.

Pizza at birthdays. Pizza after my wedding.

And now: pizza and Oona.

The combinations of pizza and people and things I love are countless. The memories are vivid and endless.

When I think about changing my diet because of type 2 diabetes it's the thought of cutting out pizza that crushes me. Then one day I have a realization: I can't stop eating pizza. But I can eat *one slice*.

This isn't based on any doctor recommendation, but it's a logic that occurs to me that the amount of bread and sauce and cheese in a single slice isn't the problem. It's the gluttony of eating eight slices that's turning my body into the size of eight people.

So I do it. I change my personal pizza policy. Just one slice. Every week. Sometimes every two weeks.

One single, dinky slice.

And I love it. I'm going to risk offending pizza purists and say I love it *more*. The idea that I can taste greatness but resist gluttony. That I can sip the richest nectar of the gods but not drink everyone's syrup.

Within six months I lose ten pounds. My cholesterol goes down. My blood sugar as well. Not where I need it to be but enough that I know I'm moving in the right direction.

I start to apply this principle to other parts of my life. I don't need to tour 112 cities. I can tour 20. Just a slice. I don't need to work seven days a week. Some weeks I can work three. Just a slice.

This is a part of a larger strategy to become a whole member of my family.

One slice.

That'll do.

As for Oona, she gets the second slice.

XII.

THE NEW ONE

WE LEARN TO DANCE

One day Jen is breastfeeding Oona and she has to pee so she hands Oona to me. The moment I take her it's like holding the angriest thing I've ever held. It's like holding my dad.

I'm thinking, *How do you think I feel? I don't know what I'm doing. I don't know anything.*

At that moment the church bells on our corner start chiming the song "Ave Maria."

Oona stops crying.

She looks up and starts bobbing her head.

I whisper, "I know. It's a classic."

Oona is transfixed. She's bobbing her head and I'm thinking, *Oona's got great rhythm. Maybe she could be a DJ or a drummer or an agreeable person. Maybe this will help her sleep and she won't need the Dream Dust or the sleep patch or the Magic Sleepsuit.*

Then the song ends.

Oona looks at me and I look at her and we both know it's about to go down.

I don't know what to do so I sing, ♪♪ *"Ah-vay Mari-i-aaa. Ave . . . Maria-ah!!"* ♪♪

But I don't know the words . . .

So I improvise to the melody, ♪♪ *"There will be a Jesus in your womb. It's actually a pretty big honor. It's more like an Oscar than an Emmy."* ♪♪

Eventually I run out of lyrics and we're looking at each other and I'm bracing myself and Oona looks me in the eye and says, "Dada." And *in that moment*...

I'm the pudgy milkless vice president with record-high approval ratings for no reason.

*

A toast to my husband

To my husband—I think he misses me. I think this because he told me. I hear him saying this. I hear him saying I said it wouldn't be like this. I hear myself saying, sorry, luv, I—

Sometimes we don't know what we need.
Sometimes we know but we don't know how to ask.

All the talking we do—and the writing—
especially the writing—
is so far from what we are meant to be doing—
which I am now convinced is dancing—

She learns to dance before she learns to speak—
And when she hears a song she recognizes
she waves hello—

We fan the air in front of our faces to say she took a shit
or to say a certain dictator stinks like maggots—

But right now, my husband is playing guitar and singing
something real stupid—
Itsy-bitsy-peek-a-boo and songs about babies
who won't sleep—

The three of us twirling like idiots—
We learn to dance before we learn to speak.

*

THE FLU

Two days after my approval rating surge I get the flu.

And when I get the flu it's worse than when other people get the flu.

I'd say a majority of my life I've felt like I have the flu. Irritable and fuzzy. My personality is sort of flu. I feel like at my funeral someone might say, "It always seemed like he had the flu." So when I *actually* get the flu, it's a problem. I feel like there's someone else inside my skin who's dead. And, by the way, that might be the case. I'm not even sure what the flu is. *Is it bacterial? Is it viral? Is there a difference? Does anyone really know the difference?* Every time someone says, "I think it's viral," I feel like saying, "Why don't you elaborate on that?" They'll say, "Well, a virus is alive." I'll think, *That might be true because whatever is in my ass is alive.*

I'm doing a string of dates in Detroit, Columbus, and then the Byham Theater in Pittsburgh. I'm backstage when it hits me. The flu is the only illness I've ever had that *hits* me. It's like being blindsided by a baseball bat and then the thief with the bat grabs your soul. When I walk into my dressing room I'm fine. That was before it *hit* me.

The moment it hits me I lie down on the floor of the dressing room and push my face up against the cold tile. I'm lying in darkness. The stage manager enters and sees me there.

"You need anything?" he asks.

"You need anything" is perhaps the most unhelpful question

one can ask a man lying prostrate on the floor. The truth is *I need love*, but I don't say that. I mutter, "I'll make it work." I roll off the floor and hobble onto the stage. I don't know what else to do. Moments later I'm looking out at hundreds of strangers. I think, *Should I tell them? What would Springsteen do? Would he shout, "This might take the fun out of 'I'm On Fire'... but my ass is on fire! Here we go!"*

That night I have a sleepwalking incident in my hotel that's so extreme that, in my dream, and—as it turns out—in my life, it causes me to escape from my fitted-sleep-sheet-straitjacket.

In my dream I'm convinced that there is some kind of government surveillance plot that has taken the shape of birds on my hotel ceiling. I get out of bed to convince the bird cameras to leave, and then realize that they aren't birds at all. They're shadows. I go back to bed and have a nearly identical dream except this time I know that the first time was a dream and the second time they are *the actual government surveillance birds* I had feared. The point is, I don't sleep.

In the morning I'm exhausted and sweaty. To make matters worse, my stomach is weak. I'm driving home and three hours into the drive I pull over at a Starbucks to—I don't mean to be crude—use the restroom aggressively. Which I believe is the rudest thing one can do at someone's place of business.

They say, "Hello, sir. We've got muffins. We can make you a latte."

I'm thinking, *That's all well and good, but what I'm gonna do is walk into that private room you have in the back and unload the most vile substance my body has been able to conjure in thirty-seven years of existence and then I'm gonna leave and I'm not gonna purchase anything and then I'm gonna drive as far away from this location as physically possible to forget this ever happened.*

But what I say is: "Do you have the code?"

I get back in the car and continue driving, now nursing a chamomile tea. I walk into our apartment after seven hours and I collapse onto our couch. Jen, who has the sweetest, most soft-spoken, thread-counted-est voice, walks in and says...

"GET THE FUCK OFF THE COUCH!"

I say, "Clo, I have the flu."

It sits there for a moment.

Jen says, "If Oona gets the flu, I'm the one who's gonna be up all night holding her until my arm is numb while my other arm is rummaging through the closets in the darkness for the thermometer and the baby Tylenol. And it's scary because I have no idea what I'm doing. And I've tried to make it so this doesn't change the way we live our lives. I don't wake you up. I change the diapers. I give her baths. But right now, you're in the way."

I start to get up.

She says, "You know that story you tell everyone about how I'm at the table breastfeeding Oona and you're doing the dishes and I say 'You're doing a great job,' and you say, 'Thanks,' and I say, 'Not you'? The only part that isn't true is that *you do the dishes.*"

I've been defeated.

I can't muster a response.

I roll off the couch and walk into my dungeon.

I lock the door. I get into my straitjacket. I can't believe my own thought.

I think, *I get why dads leave.*

THE EIGHTH REASON

I'm only comfortable writing, "I get why dads leave," because I'm not gonna leave. I love my wife and my daughter and where would I go?

Who's gonna zip up my sleeping bag?

I'm not gonna be out on the town saying, "What do you say we get outta here and you put on my mittens?"

"You mean a condom?"

"Not exactly."

I'm comfortable saying it because I'm not going to leave, but for the first time in my life *I get it*. I know that's a sensitive subject, especially if your dad left or your mom or your husband or your wife. So right off the bat, fuck them.

But if your dad left I want you to know it's not because of you.

It's because you exist.

I'll clarify that point because it's a subtle distinction. It's not because of your personality or that you don't deserve love. It's that your dad maybe didn't want to be a dad and he doesn't understand causality that well and now you're alive and I think that's great. So who cares if your dad's not around, because who needs a guy like that anyway?

That said, in this moment, I get it.

Because this person I've sworn to spend the rest of my life with, whom I've shared thousands of hours on a couch with, who has saved my best friend's life, is in the greatest love affair of her entire life, that I'm watching through a window. And all day people come up to me and say, "Is this the most joy you've ever experienced?"

And I *have to* say, "It's the most joy. I didn't know what joy was. Until now. And now I know what it is. It's this!"

I'm literally empty. Just bones and garbage and Diet Coke.

People say, "Are you full?"

I *have to* say, "I'm so full."

Which brings me to the eighth reason I never wanted to have a kid:

I never looked at my dad when I was growing up and thought, *I want to do that.*

My dad always seemed so angry. My whole life I figured maybe it was because of me or my siblings or my mom. When I got older it started to occur to me that some people are just filled with existential dread, and maybe I'm one of those people too.

Maybe I shouldn't pass that on to the next generation.

I fall asleep and I have the best sleep I've had in a year because I've accidentally locked Mazzy out of the bedroom. In the morning I open the door and smell the most heinous stench because Mazzy has peed all over the couch.

COUTZ

I'm standing in the living room across from the pee-soaked couch.

The couch is irrecoverable. I don't even think dousing it in YMCA pool water would help. I don't know what to do.

What if your cat pees on a couch? Order a pizza.

I order the pizza to distract me from my feelings but also to compete with the smell.

When the delivery guy shows up, I give him twenty dollars to help me carry the couch out to the street and that's where it dies.

After I discard the couch I quarantine myself in my dungeon for four days and on the fifth day I wake up at 4:30 a.m. and I wander into the kitchen and I do the dishes. And I'm phenomenal at it. I really enjoy it. That week Jen starts writing poems for Oona for when she gets older and I find this:

*

The Dishes

Dear Oona, in our house there is always a congregation of ants summiting around a noodle or carrying their weight in popcorn across the kitchen floor. And in the sink there is always a pile of dishes. But this morning your father did the dishes. And it made me want to fuck him.

*

I'd like to think that poem is for me.

A few hours later we take Oona to a department store and she spots this couch. It's blue. Jen thinks it's green. We look it up: lagoon. Oona loves the couch.

She says, "*Coutz!*" (couch)

"*Pi-whoa!*" (pillow)

"*Wug!*" (rug)

She's a genius.

The three of us sit on this *coutz* in the *depawtment stowa* and Oona hides behind each of us and we say, "Where's Oona? Where's Oona?!"

This is a game we've recently started playing where the premise is *where the hell is our daughter?* and the conclusion is always *there she is.*

For whatever reason, on this particular day we are committing to this game harder than ever.

We say, "Where's Oona?!"

And Oona clings to my back as I spin.

The harder she clings the more I commit.

"WHERE IS OONA?!"

I spin and she clings. I spin and she clings. And then she starts laughing so hard.

Just so hard.

It's the hardest I've ever seen anyone laugh in my whole life and I'm in the jokes business. At this idea that she's tricking us. The people in power. The people who know everything. She's fooled us completely at least this once. She's laughing so hard that I start laughing in a *new* way. From my perspective and Jen's perspective and Oona's perspective all at once.

We're laughing as one.

And, in this moment, I feel full. I'm seeing the world— through baby's eyes.

OONADAD

*

//
OONADAD

I write WALL on the wall.

I write BATHROOM on the bathroom door and CAT on the wall above the litterbin. I write MIRROR on the mirror so MIRROR appears across our faces.

My three-year-old daughter Oona cackles maniacally. Her joy of letters and language has started a compulsion in the house where we write everything on our walls and doors and windows.

I write MOM and DAD on the bedroom door and she draws a picture underneath—That's you on your wedding day. She draws a picture of herself on her bedroom door and writes her own name. On all the rest of the doors in the house I write DOOR.

Except the hallway closet where she insists on writing a double backwards HI. So: IH IH.

I write EARTH and STAR on the wall. On the refrigerator I write FOOD. BOOK on bookcase. BED on bed. SINK on sink. TUB on tub. On the wall near the toilet my daughter writes HI.

She draws a big rainbow on the hallway wall and I write RAINBOW. She traces the letters with her fingers. She draws a sun on the wall and I write SUN. On the stairs I write STEP.

If you draw a tree on the window I'll write TREE, I tell her. And we do. If you draw a hippo I'll write HIPPO and we do. She draws a mean caterpillar mommy and a mean caterpillar baby on the wall and I write MEAN CATERPILLAR MOMMY and MEAN CATERPILLAR BABY. She draws a picture of our family and says that's you in the lipstick.

I have read some poetry in my life, but the most beautiful sentence I have ever seen in the English language is written by my three-year-old daughter, Oona—in bright pink chalk on the sidewalk in front of my house—

//
OONADAD

OONA and DAD are one word, she explains, because OONA and DAD love you-ch'other. And the two little lines above it? as to offer accent or emphasis? It means they love-you-cho'ther.

*

THE BOOK ENDS HERE

Things have changed in our family. It happened over time. It wasn't a single moment but a series of moments that formed an evolution. Which brings us back to our story in Nantucket.

When Oona was fourteen months old we were in Nantucket for a film festival and when the festival director asked if I'd tell a story on a storytelling night with the theme of "jealousy," Jen suggested I tell a story about Oona.

"You're jealous of Oona," she said.

After we check into the hotel, I open up my notebook and read her a passage I had written in private.

I said, "It's almost like I didn't know what nothing was until I became a dad and then I thought—*Oh, that's what nothing is.*"

She laughed. She said, "You should say that onstage."

We were renewing our vows.

She showed me the poem that starts with "Dear Oona" about her night alone in the hospital after Oona was born. The one that ends: "she cries out, you stand, you sway you sing you feed, no matter your fresh stitches, she stops crying when you hold her, holy shit the pain, you do not let her go until morning, you wait it happens in a moment."

Some of it made me feel terrible. But I respected the honesty. And I loved the writing. Embir Bones approved.

Jen and I began sharing writing we'd done in secret over the past two years. The collaboration we didn't even know was happening.

It was often tense.

One time I showed her a draft of something I had written, and she woke me up at four in the morning and said, "If this is how you feel, then I don't even know why we're married."

At a certain point it became clear that this naive idea that we had attempted—that "this baby wouldn't change the way we live our lives"—was a lie.

We had lied to ourselves.

But not with malicious intent.

I was lying to be with the love of my life and the love of my life was lying to be with the love of our lives, whom we hadn't yet met. We were both lying to ourselves, and what resulted was a family.

That said, I will not lie about how much of a struggle it was for me to become a decent dad. But if I'm going to publish all of these raw feelings about that struggle, I think it would feel incomplete if I didn't also write this:

Dear Oona,

Congratulations.

You're four years old.

You probably won't remember this but we had a birthday party for you. The theme was "Charlie and the Chocolate Factory in space on the moon with chocolate Elsa."

I'm pretty sure you picked it.

We had a birthday party for you at two, three, and four, and we're pretty much committed to having birthday parties for you until the end of time, so you can count on it. I want you to know that I got better at being a dad. I do a lot more dishes. I'm in charge of grocery shopping. I play you guitar and we sing songs and dance. Sometimes you get in the hole in my sheet and you say, "I'm wike Daddy!" It's the best.

Sometimes when I tell people these stories onstage they say, "What will Oona think when she grows up and hears this?" And I think my answer usually surprises them.

Oona, what I want you to know is that your mom and I love you and we want you to be honest with the people closest to you. Your friends, your parents, your wife, your husband, your girlfriend, your boyfriend— anyone you feel close to. I hope that you're comfortable telling them how you feel. It's not easy to do. Because the truth is often uncomfortable. The way you really feel about things can seem unpleasant. But in my forty years of experience, I have found that it's the best chance you have to truly connect with other people.

Because all we have is each other.

I'm doing a little better with my health. I've taken time off. I've lost a lot of weight. I've dropped twenty-five pounds but my belly still makes a great drum. My doctor took my blood this week and informed me that I'm no longer diabetic. I asked him what he thinks made the difference and he said, "You chose to live."

When I was writing this book, your mother was working on her own book called *Little Astronaut*—a collection of poems. She let her family know for the first time that she is a poet. And her poems are here in this book for anyone to see. I asked her why she is no longer writing in secret and she said, "I've been so busy since Oona was born I forgot to be secret."

One of her poems changed over the course of your first thirteen months.

ACKNOWLEDGMENTS

Jen and I not only needed the eyes and ears and brains and hearts of people we respect but also of people we trust and love and to whom we felt comfortable divulging our deepest and darkest secrets.

The people who worked with us in the early stages of the book and *The New One* play are Seth Barrish, Joe Birbiglia, and Ira Glass.

When the book started to take form we expanded our circle of trust to include people who were willing to grant the ultimate favor: *to read a rough draft of a whole damn book that isn't finished and has a lot of mistakes.*

Speed Dial: Liz Allen, Rena Mosteirin, Peter Salomone, Mabel Lewis, Greg Dorris, Jonny Levin.

1st Draft Club: Chenjerai Kumanyika, Jean Hanff Korelitz, Rob Meyer, Martha Parker, Adam Leon, Josh Hamilton, James Harmon, Lee Brock, Hannah Solow, Sarah MacEachern, Josh Rabinowitz, Tami Sagher.

Wind Beneath Our Wings: Victoria Labalme, Lewis Black, Adam Gopnik, Derek DelGaudio, Chris Wink, Alan Zwiebel.

Comic Flourishes: Jacqueline Novak, Chris Laker, John Mulaney, Jimmy Carr, Judd Apatow, Pete Holmes.

Poetic Touch: Maria Garcia Teutsch, Ilya Kaminsky.

The Look: Wendy MacNaughton and Crystal English Sacca, who designed the cover.

The Feel: This book would not be possible without the vision of our editor Gretchen Young.

Smart Friends: Greer Baxter, Mark Flanagan, Dan Wetmore, Kateryna Rakowsky, Chris Sacca, Shelly Slocum, Katherine Brinson.

Consigliere: Mike Berkowitz.

Big Shots: Erin Malone, John Buzzetti and our friends at WME, as well as Kevin McCollum and Lucas McMahon and the whole team that produced the play. Also, our lawyer Isaac Dunham.

Making Books: The entire team at Grand Central Publishing and Hachette including: Ben Sevier, Jimmy Franco, Brian McLendon, Albert Tang, Haley Weaver, and Kristen Lemire. We couldn't feel luckier.

Our deepest gratitude to our parents who raised us when we were the new ones.

And to our daughter, Oona, who is the most joy.